CLIMBING WITH FATHE

A Mountain Climbing History Written by James Wynn 1896-1931

Transcribed from the Original Journal by David Walters 2012

Introduction

Of all the past times which the hardworking business or professional man finds pleasure in during the two of three weeks of his summer vacation, mountain climbing seems to me to be the most beneficial in every sense of the word. Any one who masters one of the formidable crags of the Rocky Mountains is sure to find himself raised to a higher plane of life in spirit, mind and body. His eyes become opened to the might and strength of God. At the same time he sees his own physical and moral weakness and resolves in the future to combat with life's trials and evils with increased faith and hope.

The successful mountain climber, whether amateur or expert, must be a person of a tenacious type of perseverance and endurance. No sport practiced teaches man the grit so essential to making a successful career better than this one.

The fisherman now breaks in by declaring that no avocation gives the brain-fagged business of professional man the entire rest that his does. Very true is it that no recreation is so free from exertion as fishing; in fact there is an excess of physical inaction. The banker, or lawyer, or doctor who has been bent over his des the past fall and winter, now wastes the few weeks of his vacation bent over a hook and line, not bringing into action those many muscles and organs which so woefully need it.

For another example we can turn to hunting. In this case the decay in the sportsman is not physical, as in the angler, but as we will try to show, a moral deterioration. The spirit of adventure so plainly manifest in any mountaineer is likewise to be seen in the hunter; but the spirit of kindness toward, sad humane treatment of God's wild creatures is most sadly lacking. He comes in contact with the very heart of nature, in his excursions, but alas, are his eyes open to the fact? It is seldom, most seldom indeed! His eyes are riveted on the terror-stricken form of a deer, as she threads her way through the underbrush in nervous flight. He craves her defenseless life and endeavors to protect himself by the flimsy excuse that he needs the venison for food.

It seems a pity to me that some of our most eminent men should follow this bloody path to adventure. One great ex-President is now quenching that thirst for blood in the jungles of Africa. And how many names must be written on that fatal death roll before he has drunk his fill? I admit that the so-called “man-eaters” of Africa are sometimes dangerous to the common welfare. It is by all means right to kill them when they overstep their boundaries and invade the villages. But the hunter in almost every instance does not wait for the wild animal to depart from his natural habitation and attack man; he plunges into the forest and murders the poor beast in his own household, as it were. He provokes the animal into a frenzy by torments and if by chance the beast in self-defense should kill him, it is then called a “man-eater.” As a matter of fact it is victor in a heroic struggle and if wild animals have a language of their own, then surely the stories of their victorious heroes are told to their children.

To return to my subject, mountaineering possesses the good features of both hunting and fishing, without their bad ones. The fisherman can find his beloved solitude by climbing among the peaks of “mountain land.” The hunter can here find a snowy path to adventure, that leads over the very clouds and what is better, it is not stained with blood.

Therefore, young man, you who are just beginning to get a foothold in the world, when you are able and opportunity offers, for a vacation, why not direct your attention to the hills and mountains? Tramp over the hills and dales of our own Brown County or about Brookville. It will whet your appetite for larger climbs. In the eastern ranges Mount Washington or Mount Mitchell will offer opportunity to determine the physical stuff you are made of, and your grit. Besides the invigorating atmosphere, you will almost become intoxicated with the visions of beauty and grandeur. The spirit of adventure grows upon you irresistibly and you long to scale some of the masterpieces in the Rockies, the Alps or even the Himalayas.

In these strenuous climbs one learns not only the sublimity of nature but the great lessons of life. Mountain climbing has its trials, its dangers and its failures; it has also its joys and its glorious achievements. And perhaps better than any other avocation, it teaches the lesson which has daunted so many, the lesson of *Perseverance*.

MOUNT HOOD, OREGON

Altitude, 11225 Ft.

July 1904

(Editor's note: James appears to be recollecting these stories from his youth and retelling them as a grown man. He would have been only eight years old when the following events took place.)

All during the winter and spring of 1904 the chief subject of family conversation had been our proposed trip to Yellow-Stone Park, the Cascade Range and the Canadian Rocky Mountains. Father and I had in contemplation, especially the climbing of Mount Hood. He had made it his specialty to learn from Dr. Kellogg and every other source all that he could about the different modes of ascent. Although mother laughed at the thought of us two amateurs attacking one of the Cascade Range's giants, I for my part, had always been especially partial to this feature of he trip and had inwardly vowed to at least make a desperate attempt at scaling its snowy sides.

After the tedious week of the Portland Medical Meeting was over, all was excitement and enthusiasm with the two would-be mountaineers, Father had, during the week, mounted the striking elevation in Portland known as Portland Heights and there obtained the first view of the wonderful mountain fifty or more miles away. The grandeur of the scene inspired us both and we were far from a solemn pair on Friday, the day of our departure.

After having purchased numerous camera supplies which took nearly all morning, (for father is, it must be confessed, something of a camera-crank) we managed to catch the eleven o'clock train for Hood River, a small village some sixty miles east of Portland. As the railroad runs parallel with the Columbia River and along its very bank, father was soon busy with his camera snapping the wonderful views. There are towering cliffs, and verdant groves to be seen upon this river's rugged banks, making it an ideal playground for the nature lover; and it is also an unrivalled workshop for the geologist and botanist. Here, too, the mechanic can find a dozen different types of salmon fish traps, each apparently stranger than the other in its mechanism.

Fisheries and the Columbia River were forgotten when a hollow voiced brakeman lumbered through the train sullenly proclaiming that the next stop would be Hood River.

This village, the starting point for the climb of Mount Hood, is twenty five miles from the summit. The first thing we did after our arrival was to secure a somewhat meager meal in an old rickety building, proudly designated as "Hood River's Best Hotel." After the lunch we were disheartened to learn that the daily stage coach which we were expected to take for "Cloud-Cap Inn" had left with a load of passengers a half hour before. The Hotel-keeper after somewhat of a parley with father about the failure of the stage to wait for the train, directed us to a gruff old stableman with whom we quickly made terms and were soon rattling along and approaching nearer and nearer the massive form of our goal. On and on we went by the orchards, irrigating ditches and troughs where the water seemed to be running up hill, until four o'clock, and still the mountain seemed to get no nearer. Our ride thus far had been over level country and but for the snow capped giant before us one could have imagined himself back in Marion County. To our joy, however, a steeper climb was neat at hand. The foot-hills were so near that we could trace the devious path of our road as it wound its way up among them.

Suddenly the driver reined the horses before a comfortable looking farm-house with the surprising statement that he would turn us over to another man. As he spoke the other driver appeared with two span of fresh horses and we were soon again upon our journey.

The last half of the trip was passed more pleasantly than the first for several reasons; the blazing sun had gone behind a cloud-bank in the west; Rollo, our new driver was a most sociable young student who was spending his summer vacation, driving cow-boy fashion in the region of Mr. Hood; our thirst was quenched by fine mountain spring water, and

Rollo satisfied our hunger with some luscious red raspberries which he had provided. Shortly after starting up the eight mile climb, the formidable cloud which I mentioned disappeared and lightened our fears of a stormy morrow. The sun was fast waning behind the foothills. All was silence giving the earthly fairy-land before us a solemn majesty; the mild light of the gleaming aided by the full moon, which could just be seen above the purple outline of the distant pine forests, softened the endless figures with a pale blue haze, uncertain and dream-like in its beauty. Steeper, ever steeper became the road and with the same accord, cooler and more exhilarating the breezes from the snowy banks of Mount Hood, the summit of which had become unburdened of a blanket of cloud.

Finally after a long steep climb, through the densest spruce forest, with no sounds save the creaking wagon, the horses' hoofs and the reverberating crack of Rollo's whip in the steeper places, we came suddenly into the open. The timberline had been reached and we were at Cloud-Cap Inn. The lights gleaming from the windows were a welcome spectacle to the weary travelers.

It was quite the structure I had imagined; built of rough pine logs; only one story high but long, being amply able to accommodate fifteen or twenty people. It was anchored to the ground by huge steel or wire cables to prevent it from being carried away by the strong mountain winds.

Once inside Rollo piloted us to the dining room where a dainty damsel of some three hundred pounds, after a half hour's blustering around, prepared us a meal suited to a mountaineer's appetite. It was then near ten o'clock and other guests had retired. While we were eagerly devouring the good things before us, "Pete," the guide put in an appearance, having heard that we intended to join the party for the climb in the early morning. He came to "hob-nail" father's shoes. It was then that I got the first inkling that my hopes of reaching the summit might be dashed to the ground. Pete looked me over carefully but would give no answer as to whether or not I could make the trip. He looked at us doubtfully and parried father's questions with indefinite and rather discouraging answers. You can well understand, therefore that I went to my bed with an anxious heart, but however anxious and worried, that night, if ever, I slept the sleep of the just.

The morning was brilliant and crisp as in mid-winter. Father and I went out before breakfast to reconnoiter. We climbed up on the house and gazed with enrapt attention at the snow peak just before us. We took a few pictures and then joined the merry mountain climbers at breakfast. They were a jolly crowd in anticipation of the day's adventure.

After breakfast was over, those so lucky as to possess Vaseline, greased their faces with it: others used shoe-polish, to keep the skin from being sunburned. Each carried a mountain stick except Pete who had an ice pick-axe. Trailing along single file, with Pete leading, picking our way over the rocks and boulders, we made an interesting, minstrel-like procession. Cooper's Spur, a crag about four fifths of the way up was the point toward which we first directed our course. Although it did not look to be more than two miles distant it took four hours steady climbing to conquer its summit. Our labor was amply rewarded, however, by the view which there burst upon us. The green forests below us were entirely invisible, being obscured by a billowy sea of clouds through which the summits of Mount Adams, Mount St. Helens, Mount Jefferson and Mount Rainier rose with awe-inspiring grandeur. The entire picture was almost exactly like a marine view: the clouds being the ocean and the mountain peaks volcanic islands. The only thing at this point to disturb the full enjoyment of this wonderful scene was the cutting, cold wind which came from over the vast ice and snow fields which lay upon every side of us. We could look down upon an immense glacier, in which we could see great chasms that seemed bottomless and made us tremble lest we might slip and fall into them. Pointing to one of these great snow and ice banks, the guide stated that there was where, a few years before, a novice had attempted to climb the mountain and fallen to his death. I am not sure but he told this just at this time to prepare father and me for what was coming. We climbed along the crest of Cooper's Spur till we at last came to where all signs of rocks ended and all was snow and ice. The guide then announced that it was time to "rope up" for the last stretch – about three quarters of an hour. Then came the statement of the guide that I had so long feared; he said I was too young to undertake it. Father offered him five dollars additional pay but he was still obdurate. Pointing to a huge natural rock shelter, he said I might safely wait there till the rest of us made the ascent and returned. After some hesitation father consented to these terms, and promised me two dollars on condition that I was not under any circumstances, to wander from the shelter rock until he came back. I readily yielded to the verdict, although it seemed almost like a death sentence. The two dollars were something of a solace to my wounded feelings and ambitions. I turned with tears in my eyes and beat a hasty retreat to the shelter rock. I watched father as he took his place in the line to be roped up.

This however, was the nearest he ever came to climbing that last stretch. In his fear that I might wander away he came back and no inducement would persuade him to leave me and make the climb. Downheartedly we watched the others as they slowly traced their way up the steep snow bank. Then back to Cloud-Cap Inn we sullenly trod, victims of a disappointment which waxed more bitter with each step. But one consoling thought comforted us: after disappointment and failure, success tastes more sweet. We resolved that other mountain peaks equally majestic should be the subject of conquest.

Soon after our return to the Inn a snow storm of great severity enshrouded the summit of the mountain. As we gazed at the inky cloud and the storm winds told us of the battle of the elements high up on the peak, we heaved sighs of satisfaction that we were in a safe and comfortable place. In spite of the disappointment, the experience and rewards of this climb up Mount Hood will remain "A Red-Letter Day" in our memories. After all, even the disappointment, so crushing to us, taught a lesson. Is it not true that in the most cherished undertakings of life, we often fail to attain the goal we aim at? Even Moses failed to reach the Promised Land. One's greatest reward is in the striving, if that only be worthy. He knows better than feeble man the safest road for His children.

SADDLE BACK MOUNTAIN, ALBERTA CANADA

24 July 1905

This is one of the Mount Temple Group of mountains, in the heart of the Canadian Rockies.

The traveler who has boarded a Canadian Pacific train at Vancouver and has managed to endure the long, hot ride to Revelstoke will be amply rewarded for all his past discomfort by the marvelous beauty and grandeur of the next four or five hundred miles of the road, which winds its solitary track around among a multitude of glaciers and gigantic mountain peaks, many of whose sublime summits man has never set foot upon. Hot, tired and grouchy after the first long sad monotonous stretch from Vancouver, my state in the midst of these mountain grandeurs, was now little short of hypnotic.

At the little station of Laggan , in the very heart of the Canadian Rockies, we took carriage for the hotel, or chateau as it is called, some four or five miles to the south of the railway. I sat with the driver who soon discovered that I was quite a crack on the subject of mountains. To my great satisfaction he began to give me some very useful information. Mount Temple, the loftiest and most beautiful in the region of Laggan, he declared was the mountain above all that we should try to see. A good view of the mountain, he continued, could be obtained from the summit of the Saddleback, which was four miles from the hotel. Father had, during this conversation with the driver, been apparently unconcerned, more interested in the mountain panorama about us. This opinion proved to be erroneous, however, because next day at Noon after having returned from a trip to Lake Agass, the highest of the famous "Lakes in the Clouds," he proposed making a trip up the Saddleback in the afternoon. Nothing could have pleased me better.

During the dinner hour a storm and dashing rain dampened our hopes but by two the sun shone again, and we made ready for the trip in spite of the slippery cement. Riding a mountain horse along a steep trail is not the pleasant experience you might suppose. These animals, to begin with are excessively cautious and therefore exasperatingly slow; they must, it would seem, stop and think about it before taking a step. Time passed rather monotonously on these snails of their kind. After long and laborious travel in this way we finally reached the end of the trail, where the horses were abandoned and the journey resumed on foot.

The summit which up to this time had been somewhat indistinct in outline now became plainly visible, a jagged mass of moss covered rocks looming up high above us, forming a saddle of gigantic dimensions. There seemed no chance of defeat now; nothing to hinder us (except a moderately rocky climb) from reaching the summit, not more than a half day's climb away! Crowning them all was the unrivalled monarch of the Temple Group, Mount Temple, which lay ten miles to the south and seemed to rise from the base of the Saddleback. Father secured a beautiful picture of the mountain showing the summit partly obscured by a cloud.

The name Temple is well-befitting this noble mountain for there is something strongly religious about its overpowering majesty, its perpendicular sides, its snow-rigged walls and cloud wrapped summit; an indefinable something not seen in other mountains. One with an imaginative temperament might picture it as a great natural museum, upon whose sides wondering man is shown the marvels nature there displays and is taught to revere them as monuments of God's workmanship, wrought to show how tremendous those first great convulsions of the earth's surface must have been. Entranced as I was by these surroundings my imagination had soon conjured this giant of a mountain into a core of different shapes I permitted my mind to take its fantastic course and soon all else was forgotten in an ecstasy of stupefying delight.

My mountain reveries were not to last, however; an unlooked-for occurrence brought back my senses from their dreamy flight. A rolling crash of what seemed to me the loudest thunder I had ever heard was the first warning we had of an approaching storm. Before I could cover the rocky stretch to where mother was (luckily she had brought an umbrella) the storm broke. It seemed the faster I ran the more furious the elements became! Large hail-stones mingled with icy sleet, swirled suddenly from all directions in circling clouds. These whirlwinds became bolder and after executing a number of maneuvers about my fleeting figure, directed their full fury upon it. So heartily did the hail-stones hammer my head that it was hard to believe they did not have human intelligence and had previously arranged to make it their target. It is useless for me to attempt the framing of a word picture which would describe with graphic exactitude the terrors of my dash to that umbrella. The optimism which had heretofore born me up so steadfastly, now showed signs of falling, leaving its gloomy enemy in full control. The thought that another page would be added to my book of strange experiences alone kept me from undergoing that fatal metamorphosis. But Alas! When I did arrive at the longed for destination, it was only to meet another trial even more fearful than the first. A moment after I had taken my place between father and mother under our single means of shelter, a sharp and decided electrical current shot down the handle of the umbrella. Instantly a benumbing fear laid hold of me – a fear that one of the many blue ribbons of lightening which constantly streaked the sky, might make us its victims. However the elements seemed to have seen and pitied our perilous situation because shortly after this last uncanny experience, they ceased their angry assaults, and the storm vanished as quickly as it had appeared. Once more the sky assumed its turquoise blue and the earth an emerald green. All our surroundings now took on a different aspect – one of perfect harmony, which only an evening in the mountains affords. All was quiet and serene except the mountain climbers. It was quite impossible for us to keep silent; so jubilant were we at our late success and our thrilling experiences. For my own part I was well-nigh insane with joy and enthusiasm: I had climbed a mountain!

MOUNT WASHINGTON, NEW HAMPSHIRE

The White Mountains are in my opinion by far the most rugged of all mountains lying east of the Mississippi, although the Black Mountain Range claims the honor of the highest peak in the Appalachian system – Mount Mitchell.

The Presidential Range of the White Mountains is noted because it contains the highest peaks of the system, many of them named after distinguished Americans. We visited this region early in June. At that early season only one of the large hotels was open for guests – that at Fabians', the point at which the cogwheel road is taken for the summit of Mount Washington. The "dressy" element of that hotel did not harmonize with the tastes of father and myself; so we sought the solitude afforded by the mountains and forests. Months previous we had planned that one of these mountain rambles would be a trip to the summit of Mount Washington.

The day set for the climb was typical White Mountain Day. The sun rose to find the mountains completely enveloped in a bluish haze which gave the landscape the appearance of a Japanese art panel. This fog thin as it was did not at all please father and me, for we had heard tales of treacherous fogs as fore-runners of violent tempests. However since there was enough blue in the sky to make a "whole elephant family pairs of pants" we decided to risk the weather prospect. At nine o'clock the summer resort novel readers who decked the big hotel porch (especially the dames of fashion) were probably shocked to see a homely buckboard wagon, drawn by two stalwart horses come bouncing up the road to the front steps. In a moment father and I were seated beside our brawny mountain guide who held with a stiff rein our prancing "Bengasi." During the first half hour we got a thorough toasting since the road led through an open stretch which resembled the prairies of the Middle West. Any homesick traveler from Kansas or Nebraska might easily have imagined each small snag a prairie dog and the distant mountain ranges cloud banks.

However the mountains did not long remain distant. We finally plunged into the dense verdure which covers the foot hills of Mount Pleasant. We had driven but a mile or so when the first impediment was encountered. A pine had fallen across the scarcely distinguishable roadway, very effectively blocking our progress. The underbrush and foliage were so dense upon either side as to make entirely impossible a detour at the side through the forest. For a moment we were quite dumbfounded, having no ax or saw. But the guide was not a "quitter." To our amusement he drew forth his jack knife and began hacking furiously at the limbs of the tree; then yanking them one way and another with all his might, it was not ten minutes till he had made an opening that we managed to squeeze through. Father and I were completely beat out assured that our guide was a person who could handle emergencies well. Chuckling with triumph he took his seat beside us and we resumed our journey along the rutty and grass grown roadway. This landed us finally in an old deserted logging camp. Quite a picturesque place it was – an old tumble down log stable, a dilapidated hut almost hid in weeds; and near by a rushing mountain brook with water crystal clear and cold as ice. Our imaginations pictured the sturdy lumbermen who made their abode; where once they had spent their long evenings by campfire, telling bear stories and discussing mountain fairy lore. The decaying and deserted place was now the haunt of crickets and katydids and many other species of weed-folk, singing weird songs that made one very lonesome and brought up ghosts before your imagination. The horses un-harnessed and fed; the guide disturbed my reverie by calling "Forward," and we were started upon the climb. The path circled and doubled back in a manner that would almost addle a compass. Following the zigzag trail through the mountain side forest for four miles or more, we came suddenly into the open. A sharp ascent for a half hour led us to the summit of Mount Pleasant.

At the dome like summit was a circular wall or crude tower of rock and boulders, the height of one's head – a huge coronet to which each climber had added his particular rock – crowns "Old Pleasant's bald head." In a moment I was perched upon the stone tower, gazing in amazement at the inspiring panorama, which was gorgeous but simple. The vast stretch of emerald green forest streaked here and there with yellow, was like a carpet of green velvet. Here the flight of my imagination came to on end. Frank, the guide, less given to fanciful contemplation than the rest of us, suggested that the dinner hour was near at hand. He warned us that a good three miles of rough climbing lay ahead of us before the summit was reached – the lunching place. The withering rays of the sun beat down upon us with such merciless persistency, that it seemed as though the hair would be scorched from our heads. First over the summit of Mount Jefferson, and then around the Twin Sisters we trudged. Right before us loomed up the rocky summit of Mount Washington with the Tip-Top House barely visible. The climb from here on was over rugged poles of granite. There was no definite trail visible. As we cautiously picked our way, a white cross came into view in the rocky waste. Frank explained that it marked the place where a few years before a mountain climber had broken his leg and frozen to death during a July blizzard, before the rescue party reached him. His associates almost met the same fate. I gazed a moment at the insignificant monument and then turned to the bulky form of Mount Washington which loomed up defiantly as if rejoicing over the fact that it could still claim its ghastly toll even though man had conquered its summit.

At this point upon Mount Washington the winds from the coast have a tremendous sweep, and often break upon the region suddenly and with great fury. This we had abundant proof of only a few days before when we took the cog-wheel road to the summit. A storm burst upon us as we neared the top, and so terrific were the wind and sleety rain that we could scarcely walk across from the little car to the Tip-Top House. It was a thrilling experience and impressed mother profoundly with the conviction that "we boys" should under no circumstances attempt the climb.

To return again to the tragic end of the mountain climber, we tarried a moment at the fateful spot, which made a profound impression on me, that will not be easily effaced. It emphasized man's insignificance in the face of the elements when in wrath. After all nature reigns supreme; how utterly weak and powerless is man to cope with a blizzard in the mountains!

As we clambered over the great granite masses near the top, we encountered another reminder of the awfulness of these giants. There was a pyramid of rocks and boulders, marking the place where a woman who had attempted the ascent had died of heart failure. (Editor's note: This is a remarkable foreshadowing of events yet to come in the Wynn family climbing history.) While these things gave to our train of thought rather a funereal tendency, our buoyancy and exhilaration was boundless as we reached the summit and beheld the inspiring panorama about us. If the climb had shown us some of the awful things of the mountain, it had likewise rewarded us with the joy of achieving the summit and enjoying the majestic grandeur of nature.

MOUNT MITCHELL, NORTH CAROLINA

June 17 1907

I shall always look upon my climb of Mount Mitchell in the Black Mountains of North Carolina, as more of a camping experience than a real mountain climb. Although one would expect this range to be fairly rugged it occasionally attains an altitude of 7000 feet, never-the-less, at its best it is only a wild, densely wooded ridge of peaks. The whole region is truly primitive. For miles and miles one may plod through trackless forest without a sign of civilization save now and then a cabin of rude logs.

Right in the very heart of one of these stretches is located Black Mountain, a typical backwoods village. Father and I of necessity made our way to this Mecca of the mountains, since we learned from different sources at Asheville that it was the nearest railway point to the famous Mount Mitchell, the crown of the Black Mountain Range. When our train had puffed over the beautiful Saunanoah River, into Black Mountain we alighted in the best of spirits.

At first glance things looked far from promising. The station was a rickety old shack with a considerable quota of gawking mountaineers, who kept making exclamations in a subdued tone concerning our brawn – exclamations which were disconcerting. However I puffed out my chest with a Herculean air and strutted by, utterly ignoring their insinuations. Father followed suit and together we weathered the storm f comments, until we reached the hotel. Here a supper of very plain country fare put us on our feet again, eager for the mountain tramp. After this repast we started in search of a guide, a mission which gave promise of interest and perhaps amusement.

I went along to bring father back in case of any misunderstanding with the sturdy mountaineers. The first individual that we interviewed had some vague notions about Mount Mitchell but when we questioned him about taking us up he shuddered. There seemed to be almost a superstitious fear about making the climb. "I've never been up that and I reckon I don't want to," or words to that effect. After several refusals we were finally referred to a Hugh Daugherty, who was said to have made the ascent of the mountain. Just then he sauntered up, an ancient corncob pipe protruding under a veritable Niagara Falls mustache which drooped down to his chin. He informed us that he had made the ascent some years previous and would be willing to try it again. Daugherty was minus an arm, having suffered in the late war from a Yankee bullet. We closed a verbal contract with him to drive us next morning some eight miles to the base of Mount Mitchell, where the trail began.

Daugherty appeared at the designated hour with an old fashioned, bulky one horse wagon. The same corncob pipe was in his mouth in exactly the same position that it had been the night before. From general indications I was pretty certain he had slept with it in his mouth. To tell the truth I had doubts right then about Daugherty's ability as a guide; but what else were we to do. We could find no one else who had made the climb or willing to undertake it. So we smiled and put on an optimistic attitude. Equipped with an ax, horse feed and provisions for a two days journey, our party began its journey. The lean, sharp-ribbed old fossil of a white horse meekly and cautiously picked is steps ahead, while Daugherty's twenty year old dog brought up the rear. Taken all in all we were rather a Rip van Winkley crowd. For three hours we thumped and bumped along over what was said to be a road but in fact was the bed of a creek – the Sauanoah. I never in my life saw so many boulders except along side the glaciers of the Canadian Rockies. From the noise of the rickety wagon and the shaking up that we got in riding over the boulders, we were in worse shape when we arrived at the foot of the mountain than if we had walked. But it was contracted for and we wanted to get our money's worth and the experience.

Finally Daugherty announced the end of the wagon journey. He unharnessed "Good-heart." (This is the name I have given the old horse. I don't believe that he had any name; at least Daugherty never dignified the poor brute by any reference.) We started out on foot, Good-heart now assuming the role of pack horse. For a mile or more the walk was most charming, for the path lay through a dense wood of stately trees that gracefully arched the path. Father and I were enthusiastic and kept the camera busy. Daugherty did not fully appreciate what was being done; his chief interest seemed to center in lighting and pulling at his corncob pipe. As we penetrated further and farther into the forests the thickets became more and more dense. Occasionally Good-heart owing to his ungainly stature reached impassable points in the pathway, which required the cutting away of logs, tree-tops, and underbrush. About one in the afternoon the path disappeared in briers and underbrush. After making five or six excursions in to the unbroken forest in search of the continuation of the path, and returning again to the same point, Daugherty announced that we would take lunch. While we ate he let slip a remark which froze my blood: "This here path aint the same it was when I was up here before, about twenty year ago." Father nearly choked on a rather obstreperous biscuit he was making way with and I'm afraid if I had had my mouth full still worse would have happened. However we smothered our own fears and indignation, for our only hope lay in the hands of Daugherty.

Presently through an open space in the forest he got his bearings from neighboring mountains and finally we came again upon the path much to our relief. Until four o'clock the climbing was steep but always through wooded hills where it was extremely difficult to keep bearings. About this hour we reached the summit of a mountain of foothill of Mount Mitchell bearing the romantic name of "Tater Top." When I interrogated our venerable guide as to whether the name was really "Tater Top" or the more finished Potato Top he said, "Its Tater Top; thets all I know." My query caused more trouble than I had anticipated. I was kept busy for the next half hour, pointing out stones, trees, ferns – in fact anything to hold Daugherty's attention while father had out his laugh. I cannot refrain from mentioning this incident for it is an excellent example of the scraps I usually get into on our mountain trips. It also demonstrates what a help father is in these trying situations.

After leaving the summit of "Tater Top" the trail led abruptly down. Father and I supposed that this was simply a short descent between summits. But when a half hour, then an hour and finally an hour and a half were spent in descent, father's smile began to fade. And as for mine, I had not had any for a good while. In fact I was taking every step under protest, saying we were surely going down on the other side of the mountain. In fact I was so persistent in my assertion and so firmly convinced that we were on the wrong track, that it was having an effect upon father. Daugherty, however was not to be swerved from the course. When finally we reached the bottom of the go-down, he announced that the mountain ahead of us was surely Mitchell's Peak. A mountain was ahead of us alright – about ten miles it seemed to me. I thought I noted a frown on father's face but I did not dare poke fun at him. He is a dangerous target for sarcasm in some of his moods. Besides I was not myself inclined to joke. We reached the top of this peak after about two hours of monotonous trudging but only to find that again error had been made. Later we learned that this was the summit of Klingman's peak – the rival of Mitchell for supremacy. The situation did really begin to look serious. Afternoon shadows were lengthening into those of evening; distant cloud banks converted every neighboring peak into a veritable Mount Everest. The rising might wind as it stirred the pines, shook from every tree mocking ripples of laughter; uncertain lights flickered there and there through the depths of the woods on either side of the trail. To a green woodsman even lightening bugs are uncanny in twilight. After we had gone down hill over about two miles of this enchanted ground, we came suddenly into a small cleared area where we got a view of our surroundings. Directly ahead of us lay another one of those pesky summits. "If the taint Mitchell's peak I'll give you my white hoss." For a moment my heart went out to Good-heart and I half wished we might be going wrong. For once Daugherty was right. A half hour's steep climb brought us to the top of Mount Mitchell – the crown of the entire Appalachian system. And what a disappointment it was! No tremendous chasms of jump-offs as we had seen from other mountain summits. All surrounding peaks were covered with rich green verdure, robbing them of the rugged aspects that mark for example Mount Washington or Hood in their surrounding peaks. One mountain seemed about as high as Mitchell – the mountain we had just crossed – Klingman's Peak. A curious pewter monument surmounts the highest point, where the body of Professor Mitchell lies buried. It bears appropriate inscriptions, but those who in the years past have ascended the mountain have desecrated the sacredness of the memorial. The names of many vain and foolish people are scribbled over it and more strange still it is perforated again and again by bullet marks. The spirit of chivalry which is often a Southern boast is certainly not in evidence here.

The story of Professor Mitchell's life and death is pathetic and interesting in connection with this mountain. What are now known as Mitchell's and Klingman's Peaks are in adjacent Counties of western North Carolina. For years there had been contention between the citizens of these respective localities as to which had the honor of the highest mountain. Professor Mitchell of the Department of Mathematics of the North Carolina State University resolved to settle the question. In company with his son they made at great labor surveys of the two rival peaks, finding the altitude in favor of the one named in his honor. After days of fatiguing effort in their work, they were returning to the foot of the mountain when the son went ahead to secure food and aid in bringing down their instruments and pack. Professor Mitchell remained behind to await his return. A fog settled over the mountain and in wandering about, Professor Mitchell fell over a high bluff and down upon a dead tree-top in which he was found dead. His tragic end was so horrifying that every man, woman and child is familiar with the incident.

He was buried at Ashville. But the partisan mountaineers named the Mountain in his honor and insisted that his remains should lie upon the summit. The consent of his family was obtained, and the casket was carried by relays of men to the top of the mountain, where formal interment with appropriate ceremonies was carried out. Quite a pathetic story I thought as I stood beside his simple grave, so remote from human habitation. As we stood musing in the twilight over the fate of this good man, my dreams were brought to a sudden end by Daugherty's discordant supper yell.

The lunch was quite an interesting combination. There were a few eggs which had been hard boiled, in the beginning but owing to the skill of Good-heart in rubbing the lunch sack against trees along the trail, they were now well-nigh scrambled. And eggs scrambled with the shells on do not make a very appetizing diet. When Daugherty saw our look of despair he hopefully extracted from the lunch pack a hunk of greasy bacon. That was too much. As a last resort I thrust my hand into the dessert sac, and drew forth a piece of cake – Cocoa-nut of course, the very kind I can't eat. But there was no alternative so after carefully removing all the odious strings, I gobbled it down. I could but look with envy at Daugherty as he ate the greasy side of meat and raw onions; but it did not heighten my relish for things. In fact despite my extreme fatigue and hunger I couldn't eat, with any degree of relish. Supper to us that evening was largely a farce. The thing I enjoyed above all else was drinking from a delicious spring down underneath a cliff.

Perhaps one reason why the supper was not relished was because of the prospect for the night. Of course I had never slept in a graveyard. My somewhat vivid imagination was picturing some ghostly visitations. By eight o'clock Daugherty had completed bed preparations in a little cove near where we ate supper, a pile of fir tree tops serving as a mattress and a roaring fire for a foot warmer. For four hours I slept soundly; then by fits and starts. By one in the morning I was awake. The fire was but a glowing pile of embers so it was difficult to make out the surrounding landscape. The sky only was in plain view and it did not present a very promising picture. Dense black clouds chased each other in sinister array. My heart thumped violently as I thought of what a storm would mean up there. I recalled the story told down in Black Mountain about a minister and his family who had been caught in a storm up on Mount Mitchell. It was four days before they found their way back, and the man had lost his reason. There came into my memory also the grave markers of the two men who perished on Mount Washington in a July snow storm. It is astonishing how even in the quiet environment of one's home how one will become frightened by hideous fancies of the night. Is it strange then that my imagination was pretty active and preparing me for almost anything? As I lay there watching the clouds and struggling with my imagination, something very realistic jarred my nerves. Crackling brush was distinctly audible from the direction of the summit. Some one was approaching I felt sure. With a shudder I thought of the solitary grave. Could it be that Professor Mitchell was about to make us a visit: I tried to smile at my fears but the effort was not mirthful. The mysterious somebody was coming nearer and nearer, breaking the brush with each step. I shut my eyes and listened intently till I knew the midnight visitor was at our very feet. When the suspense had become unbearable I opened my eyes looming up before us was a tall white figure in striking contrast to the black background. For a moment I thought my end had come. Then the ghostly object snorted, lowered its head and began to crop the leaves from the bushes about us. Good-heart had loosened his halter and was paying us a nocturnal visit. The remaining hours of the night were almost a continuous "night-mare." The black clouds scurried away, the wind subsided and the welcome dawn brought peace of mind. A clear frosty morning brought cheer and good spirit for the return trip, which was rather uneventful except that my overcoat was forgotten and necessitated back-tracking for a mile or more. We arrived back at Black Mountain about three in the afternoon and three hours later took a train for Ashville.

So ended my first experience as a camper and forester. The memory of it all will linger with me as long as life lasts. But as a mountain climb it will not rank with those I have previously made. Wanting are the rugged and barren ascents; seldom any great and inspiring panoramic views; but ever and always the endless forests.

MOUNT MASSIVE, COLORADO 1908

Five o'clock in the morning of our Mount Massive climb, found the sleeper side-tracked at Leadville. We had come over the mountain road from Wanitou during the night. The only passengers astir were the porter and ourselves. He spoke with the air of a physiography professor about the fleecy banks of clouds which enveloped the summits of Massive and Elbert and what the mists presaged. Our empty stomachs prompted us to break short his discussion. We hurried along a disreputable board walk skirted by still more disreputable appearing salons, until we came to what seemed to be the main street of the town. A tedious walk brought us to the only restaurant which was open – not a very inviting place but we were determined to make the most of it. We took our place among the many miners who eyed s curiously if not suspiciously. But this did not deter us from devouring the leathery steak like starving lions.

Father put to good use the proprietor's inquisitive and sociable turn of mind, by asking him if he knew anyone familiar with Mount Massive and the trail to the summit. With enthusiasm he directed us to a Mr. St. John who he said had climbed massive oftener than anyone in Leadville. Fortunately Mr. St. John was the proprietor of a livery stable only a stone's throw distant. From the name I had pictured in my mind's eye a patriarchal man with long white beard. But this like most dreams did not come true. Both my enthusiasm and hope sank as we were introduced to the real St. John – a man with a shaggy red beard, a dilapidated slouch hat, a quid of tobacco in his mouth and having the appearance of an all round tough. It was not time to quibble about appearances – we accepted him as he was – cherishing a very faint hope of agreeable disappointment.

In a half hour we were hastening along a winding road with Leadville out of sight behind and Massive looming up before us. We wended our way along the valley between the mountain ranges, passing some fields under cultivation and larger ones of ranch pasture. The general appearance was rather too civilized to suit adventurous tastes. Our opinion was soon changed however. With an exclamation our guide pointed across the field to what appeared to be a fleeing dog and said: "If I had my Winchester I'd fix that pesky coyotel." With a dismal howl it quickened its pace and disappeared in the forest. All day long we watched for other coyotes, but this wary fellow had evidently mistaken us for hunters and warned his kind to keep under cover.

After nine miles of steady driving we reached a point where the roadway seemed to fade away. It became less and less distinct and we found ourselves following a string of boulders or blazed trees, up hill, down slides and over washouts that Hoosiers would have considered entirely impassible. The road to Mount Hood could not be compared to this one; the former while steep was passable; but the latter offered all that one could desire in the form of wagon adventure. The wild dives of the wagon as it crashed over great boulders and projecting rocks, reminded one of a small launch carried up and down by the waves of a rough sea. Finally with a grand lunge, horses, rig and mountaineers emerged from the ocean of bumps upon a small level place in the forest where there were a group of rude huts. "Here we are!" exclaimed St. John, as he began unhitching the horses. While the horses were led to a banquet of tender oats, father and I stood spellbound gazing up at the mighty mountain, with its barren,, rocky, snow clad summit. There was something uncanny about the way it loomed up behind the dreamy strip of foothills. The more I gazed at the mountain, the more intense became my desire to scale its bar, rugged rocks. A moment later and we were following the lead of our guide through the forest toward massive. For hours seemingly we kept plodding our way through the sighing pines without a vestige of a trail. I was fast reaching a state of doubt as to whether I knew our bearings, when Mr. St. John announced that we were nearing the timber line and would soon begin an attack on the rocks. His predictions were verified and in ten minutes we were settling into a steady rock climber's gate. A steep rocky foothill first greeted us. Twenty five minutes brought us to its rugged top, where we expected to get a fair view of Massive. But there in front of us loomed up another just like the one we had scaled. After a few minutes rest we tackled the second and found upon reaching its summit, that it was only a bracer for another and still larger one higher up. And so one after another rugged foothill was scaled some twenty in all, until at last, we were at the final climb up Massive's summit – about a mile from the top. All had gone well thus far.

We sat down to get our wind and quench our thirst with ice cold water that trickled out beneath a cliff. Father, whose appetite had been sharpened by the mountain air, squeezed a couple of bananas from the lunch box and began munching them in a most satisfied manner. I partook also, but did not tarry long, forging ahead, anxious to be first at the top. So far I had been in fine trim, leading my companions by quite a stretch. In ten minutes after this rest I was again well in the lead, armed with a banana in one hand. Sad to relate a few minutes later, the state of affairs was decidedly different. A strange feeling, closely akin to sea-sickness had taken possession of me. Mount Massive suddenly began to perform some very complex acrobatic gyrations, plainly indicating that something was radically wrong either with the mountain or myself. As father and the guide said the mountain was right side up, I was forced to admit the fault was mine. Just as I was vainly trying to figure it all out, the two came up behind me and the guide spoke: "Ah ha! Pale about the gills are you? You ate too fast, just like all of 'em do. Better slow down and stay back with us."

After a half hour of rest we ventured to sally forth on the final stretch, but I had lost my ambition to lead. The remainder of the climb was very steep; at an angle of forty five degrees over sliding rocks. We noted our great shortness of breath on slight exertion. It was necessary to rest about every ten steps. Finally pulling ourselves up over the last rocky promontory, we were at the top. I stretched out upon a rock protecting me from the terrific wind which blew, hoping to rally from the wretched "Berg Krankheit" before I gave consideration to the panorama before us. An exclamation from father, however, brought me to my senses in spite of the mountain sickness. Crawling up cautiously from the secluded spot where I lay, to the rocks above I peeped over and beheld a view the like of which I may never see again. There was a sudden jump-off of over four thousand feet to the valley beneath with its threadlike mountain stream. Mountains towered upon every side of us, but we were upon the monarch of the group. There were the Mosquito and Massive ranges; to the south Mount Massive's chief rival for altitude, Mount Elbert; far to the north was the Mount of the Holy Cross; far to the south was the Sierra Blanca range.

The effect of this panorama was awe-inspiring. How impressive it made the lesson of Nature's majesty, power and beauty; and the everlasting endurance of the mountains. On the other hand it taught me man's insignificance and transient existence. And still more wonderful is it to contemplate the forces which brought into existence these rugged mountains. What if I did have the nausea and vertigo of mountain sickness? It was but the bitter which made sweeter the inspiring mountain view, which will hang in my memory gallery as one of my choicest travel pictures.

MOUNT WHITEFACE, NEW YORK

The day which father and I had set for ascending Mount Whiteface, did not look very promising at breakfast time. But since Mrs. Ryan, our landlady, had prepared the lunch, and on the whole seemed quite optimistic over the prospect for a good trip. We managed to get enough courage and enthusiasm to face the menacing clouds, and the sinister swish of the waters of Lake Placid.

Since the Whiteface Mountain lies at the extreme eastern end of this lake, most of the Adirondack mountaineers choose the pleasant four mile row to the mountain's base, in preference to a long round-about trail which leads one a merry chase through forests and over foothills.

Father and I had previously agreed that the eight miles of rowing should be equally divided between us; he to be the chief engineer on the going trip and I on the return. Consequently father had the first opportunity to distinguish himself as a "skipper." He performed a most brilliant chain of maneuvers which resulted in the general wetting of our boat and crew.

The real "sailing" did not begin till we reached the broadest portion of the lake near its eastern end. Here a broad strait connects the two sections of the lake; and since the winds of the south wing are always battling with those of the north, one is pretty sure to find a stiff breeze at this point. When we rounded the point it was not breeze that struck us but a miniature squall. In a moment we were rising, falling and turning around in the most disconcerting manner. It seemed as though the homely dory in its wild lunges would deposit up upon the crest of every great wave. But the appearance of the craft was its greatest and only fault; for it succeeded in "bucking" the waves in a surprising manner. It was with a feeling of considerable relief that I saw the shore nearing. Just after a gasoline launch we made our landing, father puffing and blowing quite as much as the launch.

After several expressive "whews!" accompanied by a long string of "ohs!" and "ahs" at the beautiful scenery, father seized the lunch basket and started on the trail. I was close at his heals with the cameras. The path was a typical forest trail, over hills, along rocky ravines and through underbrush. On and on we trudged but to my consternation the trail did not seem to grow steeper; indeed my ticking pedometer had registered four miles before we began to note any ascent. But when the up-hill work did set in, it came with a vengeance. It was here that our mountain training showed itself. We soon out-stripped the other climbers, notably a party of would-be mountaineers, consisting of a woman of ample proportions accompanied by several men and children. However we did not stop to prescribe for the fleshy female's short breath and streaming perspiration. She gazed wistfully at us as we tramped ahead and I fancy her secret thoughts wished for fifty or seventy five reduction in her avoirdupois.

About two hours after passing this group the timber line was reached – the place where real climbing begins. The trail at this point widens into a broad stone slide – the path of an avalanche – which seems to lead an almost perpendicular route to the very summit of White Face. It is visible for miles away as a white streak up the mountain side.

We paused a moment before starting, silently admiring the vast stretch of country which lay before us. There was Lake Placid as maps portray it in bird's eye view, an irregular and elongated body of water, with Islands cleaving its center and mountains skirting its borders. Close by was Mirror Lake bordered by hotels and white cottages. Far below we could see the corpulent lady and her companions wending their way along the circuitous path. We did not tarry long for it would not have been to our credit for such "greenhorns" to have overtaken us. We hastened to the last "stretch." When about an hour had been spent in clambering over wet, moss covered crags which threatened to leap from their treacherous foundation of shrubs and hurl us down – down – down to the distant bottom, we struck a tall ridge of rocks and bluffs, which made an easy climb to the summit.

During most of the climb the sun had beat down upon us with great intensity; there was not a breath of air stirring; and while not melting like the fat lady, we were never-the-less sweltering hot. As we neared the top the temperature changed rapidly; and as we finally scrambled over the topmost crag we were met by a terrible gale, that was quite chilling. This came from over Lake Champlain which lay many miles to the east, but in plain view.

For a half hour we stood reveling in the majestic panorama. To the east was the great Champlain, stretching beyond vision toward the north; to the west the fantastic outline of lake Placid; and Mirror Lake shimmering like a silver dollar in an ocean of green forest; and at many points, lakes none could name. But most impressive of all was the massive Mount March, thirty miles to the south a huge gray dome hemmed in by a score of lesser peaks.

"They're signaling," shouted a young man who was surveying the panorama. With that he produced a pocket mirror and began flashing the sun's rays in the direction from which the signal came. A flash was returned. People at different hotels began flashing the sun's light in answer to us. It was a novel and interesting experience.

As father and I watched these experiments in "solography," a sudden sound of puffing and blowing broke upon our ears and shattered the charm of our scenic contemplations – the fat lady had reached the top.

MOUNT STEPHEN, BRITISH COLUMBIA, CANADA

14 July 1911

In the southwestern part of Canada there is a mountainous region which many globe-trotters claim is even superior in its primitive splendor to Switzerland. The majority of people seem to be totally ignorant of the existence of such a place in America. Most Americans think that to see real mountains of snowy, rugged character one must cross the Atlantic. In so doing the traveler of course sees some of the most gorgeous mountain scenery of the earth but he turns his back upon a region quite as magnificent and much more accessible. "See America first," is a motto that is well worth living up to. The three principal gateways for exploration in the Canadian Rockies are at Glacier, Field and Logan. At Field is located Mount Stephen, one of the most imposing mountains of the entire system. This huge dome of rock looms up to a vertical height of about six thousand feet above the village of Field which nestles at its base, some four thousand feet above sea level. The front face of Mount Stephen is almost a straight wall, with numerous banks of snow clinging to depressions in the rocks. At some ancient period the whole bulk was evidently heaved up in one colossal spasm of the earth's surface. It is by far the most commanding feature of Field, with its massive, snowy summit thrust high into the turquoise blue of the heavens.

Of course all this display of grandeur was far from lost on father and me; nor did it loose its effect upon mother. But to her it only created that spirit of contentment to sit still and look up with wondering admiration. In father and me the mountain awoke entirely different emotions. The mountain climbing germ, long torpid within us began again to multiply and excite us to activity. Father's first act after arriving at Field was to hunt up the Swiss guide. This individual proved to be the genuine article – a native Swiss, who assured us that Mount Stephen was a "ferry gooood glimb." We learned that only one other ascent of the mountain had been made this season and that was three weeks previous. It took eight hours up and four hours back. Twelve hours would seem to be rather a long climb to the average individual, but it must be remembered that people infected with the mountain climbing germ have their ideas of time extremely distorted. Arrangements for the climb were made after some delay, since father absolutely refused to house his precious feet in the colossal boots offered him by Fritz, the guide. "I weel go wid no man up de Mount Stephen unless hees have nails in the shoes. Zet iss ver dangerous," declared Fritz with emphasis. Father's flowery argument could avail nothing against the bull-dog logic of the Sweitzer. His only triumph was in a compromise with Fritz whereby he agreed to have the soles of his best shoes spiked with mountain nails of formidable dimensions. My shoes had to be treated in a similar manner, but fortunately I had an old pair with thick soles. Although the shoe question was annoying in its proper settlement lay our safety; and safety is a factor which should always be reckoned with in mountain climbing.

On Friday morning we arose at three, and after breakfast with Fritz, donned our armor, which consisted of three ice axes and picks, and a substantial rope fifty of more feet in length. As we left the hotel the valley of the Kicking Horse River was still shrouded in the misty blue haze of the early morning. The sun's rays had not yet found their way into the valley but were enameling the snowy peaks of distant mountains in gold and white. It was a sight of rare, delicate beauty – a perfect color scheme, a symphony of colors the like of which no artist has ever portrayed.

The trail up Mount Stephen begins with a steep climb of a couple of miles through forest land after which it runs along the top of a ridge of foot hills. Fritz set the pace which was slow but steady and calculated to bring all the muscles into play, without overworking or straining them. By six o'clock we left the "play ground" of the climb as we entered the fossil beds, the first extensive rock deposits above the timber line. Although climbing over the loose shale rock was tiresome, we forgot our fatigue and short breath in looking for fossils of which there was an admirable assortment of the carboniferous period. About an hour's steady "pegging away" brought us through the fossil beds. Then we picked our way up a steep field of rocks from which projected frowning, precipitous cliffs, most formidable barriers. They appeared as though waiting to collapse upon some unwary mountaineer. But the vast panorama which lay unfolded beneath us after having attained their tops well repaid us for our moments of discomfort. The villages of Field appeared no larger than one's palm; and the trail over the forest foot-hills looked like a white thread tracing its way among blades of grass.

Stealthily, numberless peaks began to peer over the summits of the mountains immediately surrounding us, as though curious to learn what our quest be. As each one rose into view, from its place of concealment, Fritz seemed filled with new life and enthusiasm. As we pursued our steady way upward, he was transformed from the quiet non-committal Swiss, into a hilarious, yodeling son of the mountains.

Just after surmounting especially steep and treacherous butte, father and I perceived almost simultaneously ahead, a most mystifying object. It suggested at a glance the figure of a stoop shouldered old man with peaked hat. "Perhaps this is a mountain dwarf?" thought I to myself. Ten minutes of steep climbing brought us to the feet of the "stooped old man," but the fanciful image had vanished into a huge pile of rocks.

"Lunch break," announced Fritz.

"I suppose we only eat the first installment now," said father, rather questioningly.

"We haf been goming four hours and we ought to get to the top in three more. We had better ead something to brace us up and den it will not make us to carry so mutch."

This was quite a burst of eloquence for Fritz, but unfortunately it was not fully appreciated by his audience. Father and I were so enraptured by the vast stretch of mountain country beneath and about us that nothing so insignificant as a human voice could arouse us. However, the clink of the lunch sack as it struck the rock awoke us from our revere and we were down to earth again, willing servants of our appetites. Our preparations for starting were not so simple here as at previous stops; for not only was this, the first lunching station but also the "roping up" place.

After dexterously coiling several loops of rope about himself, Fritz made two nooses, in the rope at intervals of about fifteen feet, for father and me. These we drew taut about our waists and once more the signal to march was given. For over an hour we trudged steadily upward over a giant stair-case of buttes presenting a more serious problem in climbing than anything previous since melting snow here met us at every turn. The uncertainty under foot made extreme caution necessary with every step. Often the "Berg Stock" would sink to the hilt before anything stable was struck. Sometimes sinking to the waist in snow; again slipping, it was difficult to keep the thought out of mind that we might any moment go pell-mell over the rocks below. It was with a feeling of relief that we left the snow zone.

Henceforth the charms of our mountain climb cannot be exaggerated, by the mildest flights of the imagination; there is a sort of vague and overpowering sense of happiness which comes over one after he has left far behind and beneath him, the common walks of man. It is something akin to that inspiration aroused by an artist's rendering of a beautiful strain of music. The spiritual of one's nature completely dominates the material. So it was with me as I climbed onward and upward with naught to remind me of earth but my two companions, and the time worn crags of Mount Stephen, which seemed more a part of heaven than of earth.

At this point in our journey a frowning rocky promontory seemed to be rising higher and higher before us. Ten minutes brought us to the precipice. The wall is composed of very hard rock, extremely stratified, a fact which made it possible to scale its side. The many layers of stratus formed a natural ladder. Up over those steps we drew ourselves. The guide would climb to a point of safe footing, then I would follow the guide assisted by pulling upon the rope; then again the guide would ascent to another point of safe footing; and now it would fall to me to assist father in clambering to another cliff-step. Finally safe upon the summit of the cliff, we saw directly ahead of us the last precipice to the summit of Mount Stephen. The only way to it lay over a narrow ridge leading almost a fifty degree ascent. This ridge which was about three hundred feet long, ranged from two to five feet in width with a drop of forty five hundred feet on one side; and sixty five hundred on the other!

"You must be gareful where you steb" was all that Fritz said as he looked around at us with a mischievous twinkle in his eye. Forward we went, Fritz yodeling joyfully while father and I gazed like one hypnotized at the narrow ledge in front of us. When we were about in the middle of this bridge across eternity Fritz turned around and chuckled as he noticed the immobility of my stare.

"What de devil? Geedy? He exclaimed derisively. This was too much. I resolved to look over the ledge at any cost. There directly down what seemed to be miles, lay the distant filmy valley not marked by any distinct features, just one apparently smooth surface of dingy blue. For a moment mountains, valley and sky whirled together into a ball as I shut my eyes to rest them from the awful strain. Then I locked my teeth and resolved that if there were anything in self control I would get across that ridge. I went across and even reveled in the awfulness of the situation before we reached the end of the ridge. As we neared this point it became evident that the worst was not yet come – the final precipice, which was probably a hundred and fifty feet in height. About two feet above the base there was a ledge fifteen inches in width. When Fritz gained this point of vantage, he motioned us to join him. After waiting till I was safe at his side, he started right up the face of the cliff such as a fly climbs the wall.

"You stay there and I will see how eed izz."

A few moments later his voice called from directly above us to come on. I swallowed hard and obeyed, crawling up the face of the rock as best I could with the aid of the ice pick. Fritz all the while kept drawing my rope taut to steady and aid me. When I reached the niche in the rock to which Fritz clung, he advanced to another depression where he had safe foot-hold, and father followed coming up as I had done. After each of us had taken about eight turns at this relay climbing, we scrambled up to the final ridge along which it was but an easy climb to the summit. And what a summit it was! More like an iceberg's crest than a mountain top. Cautiously picking every step we crawled to the very crown of this grand old man of the Canadian Rockies. The panorama which lay beneath and around us has never and will never receive a true description from the tongue of man. The eye is too dazed to convey its impression to the mind; and the mind itself is confused by the magnitude of the spectacle. Six hundred snowy giants looming up far above the bluish haze of the valley – colossal statues to Time, carved by the centuries and tinged with the purest snow. What sight could be more inspiring! What must be the scenery of heaven if such sights as this are given here on earth to the gaze of sinful man?

As I stood musing a low distant whistle sounded in the valley. A train was coming. After a moment I located it, a tiny black, string-like thing, winding its way around the base of the mountains. How insignificant and feeble it did look! And how insignificant it really was compared to grand old Stephen whose foothills it traversed. Only let the avalanche sweep down the side of old Stephen and in a moment that masterpiece of human ingenuity were as naught; yet man may chisel and drill and blast its sides, year in and year out, but Mount Stephen will stand as firm and supreme as in the beginning. As it has endured the past so it will endure the future until God sees fit to pull it down – ever a memorial to His infinite, everlasting strength. Surely nowhere is the power of the Creator more plainly manifest than in lofty mountains. Those ten minutes on the crest of Mount Stephen brought me closer to God than any sermon I have ever heard. As Ruskin has truly said, "The pure and holy hills should be treated as a link between earth and heaven."

After standing for a few minutes upon the summit, in bewildered wonderment, we withdrew to a sheltered rock where we ate our lunch in silence.

The guide had contemplated a different route returning, over a great snow field perhaps coasting some. But the "bump of caution" was large because of a narrow escape he had three years ago in Switzerland. He was with a party of nine in the Alps on a great snow field when they were carried down by an avalanche, which killed five of them, maiming him. Hence he advised returning by the hazardous rock route rather than risk the snow field.

Returning it fell to father to lead the way. He did splendidly until we reached the terrible ridge described in the ascent, when his legs seemed to melt under him at the critical point, and he straddled the ridge. A little rest however, seemed to restore stiffness to his limbs and courage to stand upright, and we journeyed cautiously on, arriving at Field at three thirty, leaving there by train an hour later.

So ended the greatest mountain climb I have ever taken. But the ending of the climb does not end its benefits. Not only as a golden leaf in memory will I treasure it, but also as an encouraging remembrance for the future. For that God who led me through perilous paths, over yawning and frightful abysses to the crest of Mount Stephen and back again to safety, will surely not desert us in the trials of everyday life.

OUR TRIP THROUGH GLACIER NATIONAL PARK, MONTANA

August 1912

Although it has doubtless been said that the Great Northern Railway directors have adopted the Glacier National Park purely as a money-making proposition, it cannot be denied that, whatever the cause of the so-called adoption, its results are in every way beneficial. It marks another step in the noble work of developing America's scenic wonders, which though quite as picturesque as much of what is called Europe's best, are still shrouded in a haze of ignorance. Previous to the last decade, the beauty spots in our own United States (that is the truly rugged mountain beauty spots) were the haunts of trappers alone, and occasionally a courageous nature lover or geologist. And all the time these beauties of the wilderness lay but waiting the exploration of the many tourists, they were delving in the splendor of the Alps, Andes, Himalayas, Arctic's – in everything but the mountain fastnesses of their own United States. The large percent of them were unquestionably ignorant of the existence of surpassing scenery right here in our states, even ignorant of the whereabouts of Uncle Sam's National Parks. But what is even more to be deplored, this ignorance is not only a thing of the past, it exists today. Seven people out of every ten cannot now write one sentence giving but one item of first hand information about, say, Estis Park or Glacier National Park. Nor can they be blamed for their ignorance. Travel resources have been such that exploration of European mountains has been almost easier than that of American mountains. With such a state of affairs existing, is it not praiseworthy for a railroad company to attempt to develop the wilderness so that American people may see the most matchless piece of mountain scenery in the United States? The author can think of no more fitting way to close this little introduction than by expressing, not alone for himself but for the others in his party, his respect for and appreciation of the work of Mr. Louis Hill of the Great

Northern; for had it not been for Mr. Hill's laudable efforts in opening the park, the author would probably never have had the opportunity of penetrating the hidden beauties of the place.

Chapter I

Our traveling party was not very large. It consisted of the three of us Wynn's – the hardened globe-trotters, - and Miss Carrie Hyatt, a pianist whom Chaminade and the big "bugs" have been avoiding for years. But human beings were the most insignificant item of our party; at least, so the average individual would have thought to see us coming down the street. We were the bane of existence to street car conductors and Pullman porters for; fully equipped we carried eight valises of various sizes and descriptions. Just how two ladies and two gentlemen can manage eight articles of luggage without the ladies becoming full-fledged suffragettes may at first appear to rival a Chinese puzzle. However, a satisfactory arrangement was made, although I doubt not it was the source of quite a material loss of weight on the part of the gentlemen. But despite our formidable outlay of baggage, our traveling party (that is, the part that could appreciate the scenery) was, I repeat, small. Probably at this juncture, the reader will question how four people (three claiming to be traveling experts) could manage to think of articles enough to necessitate the carrying of eight valises. I confess that this question is beyond my power of explanation; it baffles me, as indeed it must any mere man. Suffice it to say that two of the party were women. Such an explanation has accounted for even more prodigious occurrences. I trust it may serve the purpose here.

At quarter of ten on the night of June thirtieth, the Oriental Limited pulled into Belton, Montana, with our party, wide-eyed and breathless, waiting in the Pullman vestibule, fortified behind a breastwork of baggage. When the long line of cars finally came to a standstill, we scrambled off, and George, the porter, by quite an elaborate series of gymnastic maneuvers, landed our luggage before the train started. After calling the valise role we proceeded to the hotel where we spent the night.

The Belton Hotel (I capitalize the "h;" for it is the one and only one) is on the installment plan. It is composed of a number of picturesque log chalets of Swiss architecture. These are scattered about the bases of the Belton Bluffs, a ridge of wooded, rolling hills very similar to the Black Mountains of West Virginia. The little chalet village with its terraces, is very dainty in its beauty, but it little hints at the wonders which lie within the park.

The next morning, the Wynnses' specially conducted party took the stage (a modern one) to the foot of Lake McDonald. The drive is about two miles and a half in length and it is through the densest kind of fir forest. The traveler who has not been west can have no conception of a primitive mountain forest of the Rockies. In this particular region, the trees and shrubs must have come to an agreement to exclude the rays of the sun; for they co-operate very effectively to preserve eternal night within the forest depths. As we bumped along, only the trees bordering the road were visible. All attempts of the eye to penetrate the depths were futile. The farther back the tree, the dimmer its stately trunk until finally all faded into opaque, impermeable blackness. Almost all of the road lay through this somber wilderness of verdure. Then, as suddenly as we had entered, we emerged, on the very shore of beautiful Lake McDonald. At first glance, the lake appeared to be about a mile in width and two miles in length, but the distant mountain range at its head belied this deception. There was an unmistakable blue haze veiling the peaks, which plainly bespoke the lake to be nearer ten miles in length than two.

When we had boarded the launch, the strange tourists began to rave extravagantly about the beauty of the scene. The placid blue surface of the lake stretched far in front, gradually fading into the filmy purple of the mountain range. But I could not go into ecstasy over the view. It was a very charming one, no doubt; but it lacked the rugged, gigantic grandeur of high mountains. Then, too, there was no snow visible. As the land slid away in our start for the head of the lake, Glacier Hotel, the tantalizing fear kept haunting me that we might be entering an Adirondack resort instead of a Rocky Mountain playground. When we reached the hotel, matters looked no more encouraging. There were rocky mountains, but still no snow.

The rest of the day was spent by each as he chose. Father and I took a four hour "hike" up the Sperry Glacier trail, and our respect for the mountains grew very materially. The girls slept and rested until suppertime, after which formal activities were once more begun. The opening feature of the evening was a row on Lake McDonald, during which father went through the motions of fishing. Fortunately for his reputation as an angler, the girls, who were with us, conceived the idea that certain little rippley spots on the lake's surface were whirlpools because of a queer rotary motion of the water. Consequently, they determined to return home, and since Miss Hyatt was one of the "hands" at the oars, the mere men of the party were forced to acquiesce. Father, to this day uses this premature return home as a varnish to mask his own greenness as a fisherman.

No sooner had we pulled up at the hotel dock than a cowboy in dress costume introduced himself to father and began to sing the praises of his horses with a tongue quite as capable of rapid action as his six-shooter. Although his officiousness made him thoroughly disagreeable from the tip of his red nose to his raw-hide shoes, he seemed to have the best horses, so he was finally engaged to take us to Avalanche Basin on the morrow.

For an hour or so later, we listened to a husky old trapper, tell bear stories and then we "turned in" to sleep the sleep that mountain air alone affords.

Chapter II

The next morning seemed half-hearted about coming, and even when it did conquer the night gloom, it did not enjoy a dazzling triumph. When I had donned my elaborate (but inexpensive) mountain clothes, I hastened to the end of the launch dock, resolved to drink in the fresh morning air as an appetizer for breakfast.

The spectacle that the lake presented was at once ominous and beautiful. Its waters were a placid grey that ran into the murky sky without perceptible dividing line, for the mountains at the head of the lake were totally lost in mist. Farther down toward the lake's foot this mist gradually took the distinct form of fluffy, cumulus clouds. One of these, just discernible in the distance, hung so low, that it resembled a great, snowy wad of cotton, floating on the water. Although the sight was fascinating, it did not portend a very favorable outlook for us Wynnses; for it is a mountaineers' adage that low lying clouds foreshadow mountain squalls, and these squalls are certainly not of a mild variety. But I did not worry long. The breakfast gang considerably disturbed my unpleasant meditations and I "joined the happy throng" at the door of the dining chalet.

It is surprising what a prompter of optimism such plebeian articles as ham, eggs, and porridge are. After stowing away a disgracefully large amount of each, I rose from the table, endowed with new life and enthusiasm, ready to face all weather adversity and a few wild things besides (at a safe distance). As I intended to tramp to the Basin, I inquired the trail and started somewhat ahead of the other three who had planned to make the twenty mile trip on horseback. (To him who has read the previous chapters of this book, it may seem strange that father would consent to such an easy means of transportation as horseback riding. It was by no means a case of "cold feet" on his part, but one of blistered feet. On the previous day's tramp up the Sperry Glacier trail, he had experienced his first brush with mountain shoes. In this primary encounter with the raw-hides, he had been clearly worsted; his whole bearing whenever he did walk on the day of the Avalanche Basin trip was that of a man walking on hot irons.)

After I had threaded my way by means of blaze marks and horse tracks, through the forest for about half an hour, the sound of heavy footfalls on the soft moss of the trail made it evident that the rest of my fellow-travelers were at hand. I stepped to the side, thinking to let the "stately" procession pass that I might follow more leisurely in its wake. But the guide's horse alone availed himself of the opportunity to get ahead. The others were so far behind that I fell in line behind the leader, not waiting to become the caboose (or shall I say observation car) of this slowest of freights.

During the early part of the morning the trail came into the open but once, and that was on the banks of McDonald Creek at the falls. This cascade is picturesque, but more like a lowland waterfall than the giant cataract of Takkakah, in the Canadian Rockies, of which I had hoped to find a rival. As I look back now on this occasion, the feature which stands out most prominently in my mind, is father's matchless operation of his "forgettory." In the short ten minutes we spent at the falls, he managed to lose and re-find his fishing rod (the latter, not until he had created consternation among horses and riders.)

Several hours after leaving the falls, we came upon a little mountain torrent that has left an ineffaceable impression upon my memory. Fairy Gorge, the guide called it, - and well it deserved the name. The stream had evidently been following its present course for many centuries; for there, in the very heart of the woods, where the sun's rays became a dull, soft radiance, it had washed out a terraced channel from seventy-five to a hundred feet in depth, from the solid rock. At the bottom of this "canyonette," its foamy blue water tumbled down, down, down, finally losing itself in depth and mist. Nature had judiciously softened the sternness of the gorge's sides by draping them with olive green moss and fern. For some time we sat by the trail on a velvety cushion of this same kind of moss. We doubtless would have idled the rest of the morning away in that same spot had not Harry, the guide, aroused us. Mechanically, we got up and continued on our way, dazed and stupefied. But father and I were not so overcome by the soporific qualities of the place that we forgot our cameras. After the guide and the girls had gone ahead, we stopped a few moments to give our time to snapping the shutter. The pictures have proved to be very inadequate. They so belittle the charms of Fairy Gorge that we have discarded them. (Such disappointment is one of the bitterest dregs in the photographer's cup of woe.) Now the only record we have is the mind's eye picture. And alas, how hopeless a task it is to describe that "film" to a stranger to the original!

From the gorge, the trail was all a stiff upgrade so that I soon found myself puffing in my constant effort to keep up with the horses. But soon there came to the rescue that priceless treasure of the athlete and mountain climber, - second wind; and with it came a delightful surprise I little had counted on. When I became conscious of a lightening in the sky as though the storm clouds might be going to blow over, I took the liberty of pausing to rest my travel-accustomed eyes and to survey the situation. As my eyes followed the rocky summit of the mountain directly in front of us, I discovered the massive, snow-capped top of a real alpine peak looming up behind! My eye, once having made the discovery, was trained for others and before long it had sighted seven snow-covered monsters, peering at us like so many giants from their invulnerable fastnesses. These discoveries sent the blood surging through me with a thrill and the mercury in my good cheer thermometer went up with a bound.

The trail details of the rest of the trip I cannot recall. While before I had marked each new phase of the trip with unerring accuracy, after my discovery of real mountains, such trivial matters as trails and the like became entirely too insignificant for notice. During the rest of the tramp to the Basin, I continued to gaze skyward although it caused me a number of disconcerting stumbles and near falls.

We reached the shore of Avalanche Lake about noon in the midst of a drizzling rain storm. This was especially disappointing, since we could get only the most vague ideas about the lake; but even what we could see plainly indicated the body of water to be well named. It appeared to lie at the bottom of a huge basin, the rim of which was unbroken on all sides except the one through which we had entered. Over one side of this perpendicular wall, four, three thousand-foot waterfalls tumble into Avalanche Basin from Sperry Glacier which is just above the rim. The guide told us that from one portion of that same ridge, the pinnacle of the Little Matterhorn rose four thousand feet above us. The real Matterhorn itself might have risen from that ridge without our knowing it; for the murky cloud-banks obstinately refused to lift.

A few moment s later we returned to the shelter of some underbrush just a step from the lake shore. Here the guide boiled coffee and we ate our lunch. Since it was drizzling and none of us were overstocked with clothing, we started back as soon as lunch was eaten.

How different everything was going back! My seven mountains were so completely hidden by mist and rain that I felt half inclined to believe my seeing them had been but a dream. The trail had degenerated into a swamp, the black mud of which was so find of embracing my mountain shoes that several times I was in imminent danger of floundering. The aforetime beautiful Fairy Gorge was so black and its waters thundered so that it might well have been taken for a back door to the Inferno. In short, the settling storm made the return trip anything but promising.

But entertainment came to break the monotony, and from an altogether un-looked-for source, - the girls and their horses. Mother rode a large, muscular animal named Helke. Just how the poor creature fell heir to this title, even the guide, confessed his ignorance. Helke, however, seemed to appreciate his responsibility and the necessity of bearing up strongly beneath his name; for he stopped very frequently to rest or refresh himself with horse dainties of the wayside. These stopovers became so frequent that mother became quite incensed and made the very forests resound with the name of her wayward steed. Now the reader can readily appreciate what the word Helke might sound like to a listener three hundred feet away when shouted loudly by an irate female. I was that listener! – My one consolation was that no minister graced our party.

The Chaminade rival contributed to the amusement program by losing her "slicker" (rain-coat). This feat she executed very readily, for she carried it thrown over behind her saddle. Consequently she can hardly be blamed for not being certain of the whereabouts of her slicker; for gazing at the saddle back is not a gyration which many amateur "cyusse" riders care to attempt. The first time it slid off, the horse stopped so often to look back after it that it was missed almost immediately. But the second time it didn't happen so fortunately. Miss Hayatt was too much wrapped in watching mother's maneuvers with delight to notice her own horse's warnings when the slicker fell off. As a result the guide had to ride about extra miles when the loss was finally discovered. The cause of the whole affair was duly christened "Slicker Carrrie."

After this brilliant performance on the part of Miss Hyatt, mother felt called upon to execute one grand climax act with Helke. Accordingly, when she had ridden an unusually long stretch, she complained to Harry that she was becoming weak in the knees. (The good English usage is meant here; not the slang phrase.) Mother evidently felt sorrow for having called Harry's attention to such a trivial matter as her own bodily discomfort, for she immediately started to dismount without his help, apparently wishing to make amends by not asking his help. But alas, her altruistic deed of self-denial did not end as gloriously as such events are wont to turn out in novels. She easily got one foot out of its stirrup and threw it over the horses back, but here her heroism met its first check. The obstinate slicker had so draped itself about the saddle-horn that she could get neither up nor down. So there she hung quite helpless, adhering to the fat side of her steed, who had turned his great head and was gazing at her with an expression almost human in its drollness. The tableau was indeed enough to make a horse laugh. Harry came to the rescue after indulging in a momentary spasm of giggles, and my bewildered mother was escorted earthward from her elevated position. It was of course Miss Hayatt's turn to laugh, and right well she availed herself of the opportunity, Mother thereafter knew no traveling title but "Saddle-horn Maw."

Our bedraggled but cheerful squad filed into the hotel environs just in time for supper. There were no nocturnal musicales of after-supper rows that evening. We all meekly went to bed almost as soon as supper was over. Twenty miles of mountain hiking surely is a great cure for insomnia.

Chapter III

Although the fates seemed against our little party with regard to weather, they certainly favored and compensated us for this impediment, They left within our reach one of the best guides in the park, - Mr. Goe. H. Jennings, of Midvale, a trapper who has hunted and tramped in Montana, Idaho, and Wyoming all of his life, who knows the Rocky Mountain passes and ranges quite as well if not better than we the sidewalks of our city streets. Perhaps the most pleasant attribute of Mr. Jennings is his versatility. Although a thoroughbred mountaineer, he is a cosmopolitan enough to shift his point of view and look at the scenery through the eyes of the particular party he is conducting, whether it be a party of "New Yawkuhs" or a crowd of western "cow punchers." This attribute of course renders him invaluable as a guide and companion; for he is not the least inclined to make jest of ignorance, but rather to dispel it by good-natured explanations from his surprising store of self-acquired nature knowledge.

Mr. Jennings arrived at Lake McDonald with a party from over the hill (Lake St. Mary's) on the same evening that we straggled in from Avalanche Basin. His party was so enthusiastic about him that the merits of Jennings were the general topics of conversation among them that evening. Father was not slow to make their acquaintance, after which he gave them a mild for of cross-examination on the subject of Jennings. The result was so gratifying that father lost no time in negotiating with the much-admired subject of the conversation, to the great disappointment and rage of our friend Higgins (the gentleman of the red nose and raw-hide boots) who had been dogging us quite as persistently as he had on that first night. Mr. Jennings was engaged though, and father and I immediately returned to inform the girls.

The girls were not in an altogether optimistic frame of mind. Miss Hayatt had wrenched her ankle, and mother, quite out of spirits after her continual misunderstandings with Helke, was on the confines of distractions because Mr. Jennings had told us that only baggage light enough to be carried, or thrown over the saddle could be taken. To sort out our necessaries from our luxuries and to pack the former into suitable shape for "roughing it," and the latter for train shipment to Midvale, mother declared would be an all night task. But after a good deal of quick work on mother's part and quick, blustering mixing up of material by the mere men, the "all night's task" was accomplished in about an hour; and we filed off to bed, having first decided that father and I should start on foot early the next morning for Sperry Glacier Camp, leaving the girls and Mr. Jennings to follow with the horses at noon, after a good morning's rest. As I lay wrapped in my blankets, I could not help shivering as I thought of Miss Hayatt and her sprained ankle, as I heard the discouraged sighs of Saddle-horn Maw.

Father and I rose quite early and stole from our bedroom like two thieves taking French leave of a penitentiary. There really was no need of this precaution, as we found out later, for almost every one was up but our own girls. Somewhat disgusted at having our glory as early risers this lessened, we gobbled down breakfast and immediately set out on the familiar trail of Sperry Glacier Camp.

The trip from Lake McDonald to Sperry Camp is the most tedious in the park. All the six miles of the trail are steep uphill and through very heavy timber. The climber continually becomes winded so that more than a mile at a stretch is torture. Even when we paused to rest, there was no refreshing snow-borne breeze to renovate us, only the sweet, languid sadness of the pines moaning. Despite the little stretch through the open just before reaching the camp, the trail cannot be said to compare with the others. It is the work that precedes the play, the labor before the enjoyment.

As we plodded along, wondering how this lap of the journey would affect the girls, half fearing they would be inclined to turn back, one of us hit upon the idea of indicting missives to the girls. Immediately my new loose leaf note book was dedicated to the purpose; its leaves were inscribed with some pertinent messages (some in verse; others in prose) which were attached to conspicuous twigs along the wayside. All of these notes were of the cheer up!! variety. We prided ourselves on having thought of this ingenious method of appealing to the disconsolate females at the psychological moment, but I have my doubts, now whether the notes were not of more benefit to us weary pedestrians, than to the girls.

When we had arranged about six of these epistles at intervals of about a mile, we found ourselves at Sperry Camp where the familiar tone of the dinner gong (same style of gong is used at all the camps) attracted us to the group of portable tents with an irresistible magnetic influence.

Sperry Camp is very picturesquely located. It lies in the bottom of a basin through which Sprague Creek flows on its way from Sperry Glacier to Lake McDonald. Directly north of the camp rises a steep ridge very similar to the Avalanche Basin, but not so precipitate. The western end of this ridge continues back into the mountains, forming a spine of Mount Edwards. To the east it loses itself in the barren walls of Gunsight Mountain, which frowns on Sperry from its lofty station. By all the natural laws of mountains, there should have been a lake where Sperry Camp is located, - a lake such as Avalanche, - but (probably just to baffle geologists) Dame Nature has drained the place "fry as hay" through the agency of Sprague's Creek. Where a placid sheet of water apparently ought to be, there nestles the tiny group of tents, rendered all the more picturesque through the uniqueness of its situation.

Immediately after dinner, father and I started up the Sperry Glacier trail to spend an afternoon which we may look back to as the most remarkable one spent in the park. For an hour or so we followed the circuitous path which leads to the summit of the ridge, behind which is Sperry Glacier. Up, up, up, - over loose shale rock which rendered climbing almost as useless as walking on a tread mill. But this steep, unpleasant work was not without its particular reward. We ascended with such directness that we soon were above the mosquito zone. At Sperry, the little aerial pests were as "thick as hair on a dog's back" (the camp foreman's expression); so we were by no means sorry to part company with them. I must confess our relief at leaving the bug region quite overshadowed our sensations of delight, more directly attributable to the grandeur of the scenery.

But our frivolous enjoyment and merriment over such a trifling matter as the absence of mosquitoes, was short lived. Coming suddenly to the summit of a little terrace in the cliff, we were confronted by a sight which of its kind is surely an unrivalled gem. No grand expanse of mountain and glacier, no terrific precipice to sicken the mind and terrify the nerves; just a fair lake! Nor do I use the adjective in a loose sense, for it was with the feeling that I beheld something supernatural – a mirage- that I gazed and gazed. There are times when we all are conscious of a vagueness, an unreality about what we see. Survivors of horrible accidents often tell of an unearthly atmosphere enveloping their environments as the crash came. They declare it all seemed but a dream. In quite such a state was I, but it was occasioned, of course, by no calamity. The whole landscape seemed wrapped in a mist of unreality. I seemed to gaze on a gem of Elysium which my eye had no right survey. The surface of the lake seemed a shimmering nothingness, so limpid was its margin; but, like a morning glory, it deepened to the richest shade of blue in the center. Verdant fir and pine trees, all bowed in silent admiration, dotted its bluffed shores, and at its far end a monstrous snow drift of spotless white rose from its craggy shore, like a hoar headed patriarch of the highlands guarding his child. Soft, velvety grass, (the kind wild goats feed on) gave a gentle finish to the bare rocks and added a final touch to the already perfect beauty of the spot. We allowed our thoughts to descend to earthly things only long enough to operate the camera. It proved of no avail. Now my suspicion that there was something supernatural about the little lake has proved to be fairly reasonable, for the pictures of it are grotesque splotches of contrast that look quite as if some goblin finger had rubbed off great streaks in an effort (quite effective) to make the camera useless.

We lingered till the lengthening shadow of Mount Edwards warned us to move on, - to come upon new wonders of natural handiwork. The first of these was a graceful ptarmigan of the grouse family. She was very sociable and thoroughly feminine in her loquacity. She had a little family with her about which she was continually expostulating, evidently telling us what beautiful speckled brown grouses her children would be during their summers of maturity, and how well they would look in their winter attire of white. We hurried on, much edified by this information, but much more delighted by a second terraced lake much like the first, which we had passed in the interim.

Finally we found ourselves climbing up the final ledge, holding our breaths in earnest expectation. On reaching the top, we were on Sperry Glacier, which comes quite as close to the basin edge as water to the rim of an overflowing glass. A stiff breeze was sweeping the ledge with an impetus that soon relieved my clothes of all surplus dust, and my mind of its feeble wits. I went striding along the snow-neve of Sperry, vociferating like a lunatic. (Perhaps I was one, for mountains are my monomania).

But once in my life have I seen a mountain panorama that equaled the one from Sperry in enormousness or beauty. To the northwest stretched a great chain of ridges and peaks, the farthest of which were well up in the Canadian Rockies. Among the nearer peaks, old Cleveland and Heaven's Peak stood with their giant heads silhouetted against a dazzling background of cumulus cloud. (Cumulus cloud is especially common in Montana because many of the United States' worst storms originate there.) Far to the southeast, the giant Going-to-the-Sun lifted his huge, rectangular block of a head high into the clouds, while still nearer than the little Matterhorn (which rose but a short distance ahead from the base of Sperry) were Gunsight Mountain and Mount Edwards with their great backs against Sperry Glacier, like two huge refugees from Hades, striving to cool off after centuries of baking.

We tramped about the snow-neves of Sperry, constantly snapping the cameras, until the sun disappeared behind the dark summit of Mount Edwards, and an increasing chilliness in the breeze told of the approach of night. How gorgeous must be a night on Sperry Glacier! I can well imagine it with the billion stars of a sable sky reflected with a multiplicity of brilliancy by the glacier and the tiny diamonds of the snow-neve. Only let the rising moon silver the stretch of mountain and cloud: we should have perfection, beauty of the purest sort.

But of course being unequipped with camping necessaries, we could but return as we had come, to gaze upon familiar beauties touched with the added charm of dusk. The little grouse still chatted of her family as we passed; the delicate beauty of the lake still appealed to us as it slept beneath the watchful eye of the patron snow-drift. The tiny tents still nestled in their accustomed places. All was the same except for one change. Two yellowish particles before one tent reminded us that the girls might be waiting for us. Presently the two yellowish specks began to take on the appearance of two females in divided skirts, and a moment later a gyrating white speck above one assured us that they were our girls and that they had sighted us. We quickened our pace until we fairly charged down the slopes at fully five times the pace we had ascended them. This hasty trip did not make our arrival at the camp an untimely one; for just as we crossed Sprague's Creek which runs in front of the camp; the dear old clang of the supper gong greeted us.

We had a lively time at supper talking to two young ladies who were the proprietors of the camp. They were sociable and cordial, yet withal so refined and cultured that we were quite charmed with them. Our girls were in the best of spirits, their only regret being that they had not been able to include the Sperry Glacier tramp in their itinerary. Their regrets were by no means uncalled for. I shall always count Sperry Glacier climb one of the "red letter" trips of my life.

Chapter IV

With this trip I approach the most eventful trip which our party, as a whole made through the Park – the crossing of Lincoln and Gunsight Passes. It cannot be said to compare with parts of the Sperry Glacier climb from the standpoint of sheer beauty, but it is surely a good display of the stupendous, gigantic elements of mountain scenery.

At the advice of Mr. Jennings, father and I started a half an hour ahead of the horse section of our party, for the horses very easily overtake the pedestrians here because of the steepness of the trail. It was quite such a morning as the one on which we had started for Avalanche Basin. Mount Edward and Gunsight were both choked in clouds, and a fitful breeze occasionally disturbed the tree tops in its uneasy meanderings. Lincoln Pass, which lies southwest of Gunsight Mountain – between that peak and Mount Lincoln, was darkly shadowed by a low-hanging cloud, but a radiance about its edge gave evidence of the sun's rise.

The entire aspect of Lincoln Pass and the winding trail that zigzags up its bare sides, finally disappeared over the crest, reminding me of an illustration I had once seen in an ancient copy of "Pilgrim's Progress!" The path looked hard; the slope barren and desolate; the summit craggy and forbidding. But behind the sharp, black outline of the ridge crest, there appeared a glorious radiance in the sky that belies all description.

As we "pegged" along in steady swing, my imagination so ran wild that I soon found myself in a tremor of expectation as we neared the wall's top. The summit was finally reached after a little burst of speed from which I could not refrain, although I knew the impropriety of such action from the mountaineer's standpoint. The ledge was truly a ledge, by no means such a plateau as we had encountered Sperry's rim. The stupendity of what lay beyond totally stunned my senses. I could almost hear my brain's incredulous laughter at the extravagant "nervograms" sent to it from my eyes. Such a scene as that was, usually affects the climber in one of two ways: either by making him miserably sick, apprehensive that he is about to fall an infinite distance to and through the depths of perdition, of by rendering him insanely stupid of foolish. It affected me in the last mentioned fashion. I stood blinking at the stupendous panorama before me, much like a harmless, good natured maniac. About a mile and a half up, rose a tremendous ridge, much higher and steeper than that of Sperry Glacier – so steep that doubtless its only climbers are wild goats. The sheer face of this wall was corrugated in places so that the otherwise barren precipice was here and there flecked with snow and ice banks which ranged in size from mere drifts to medium sized glaciers. This mottled grey and white effect lent an Alpine tinge to the whole, which is invaluable as a beautifier of any mountain scene.

This ridge continues to the northwest to form the main spine of Mount Jackson, the giant of the region who lifts his massive head almost a thousand feet higher than even the summit of Gunsight Mountain. Mount Jackson is a peak noteworthy not alone for its great height (second highest peak in the Park) but also for the magnitude of its bulk. It is the mother mountain, about which the others nestle like so many chicks. The summit of the mountain is large – but large with respect to length alone; for, though the summit is a hundred feet or more in length, it is a ridge, both sides of which are perpendicular. There is very little snow near the summit on the front face, but lower down, the steep, crevasse-scored surface of Ellsworth Glacier stands out in bold relief. So Mount Jackson towered before us in all his splendor, for the first and last time. (I trust the reader will pardon my digression giving this some what detailed description of Mount Jackson. I feel licensed so to do because this was our only opportunity to see Mount Jackson as a whole under favorable conditions.)

But the mountain features were perhaps overshadowed by some even more memorable additions. The multitude of snow-banks and glacierettes had not been distributed on Mount Jackson ridge for no purpose. Each one had its particular contribution to make in the formation of a lake which lay at the ridge base – between the Lincoln – Gunsight and Jackson ridges. I am frank to say after eight years of rather extensive traveling throughout the United States and parts of Canada, I have never once encountered a lake that combines the elements of stupendity and also delicacy of beauty so effectively. Lake Louise – so it is named – is absolutely unique in one respect. It is usually the case with mountain lakes that they are situated at the base of range foothills. Here the very formidable slopes of the Jackson ridge itself form the shore of Lake Louise. Still the light blue surface of the lake (a mile in length and a quarter in width) ripples innocently in the breeze, quite oblivious of the fact that an avalanche from the frowning heights of Jackson might fill up her smiling depths in almost the twinkling of an eye. The southwest shore of Lake Louise is a ledge, the base of which is fifteen hundred feet below the level of the lake. Over this precipice a waterfall tumbles recklessly to the distant bottom, there forming a tiny blue bubble of a lake – the little Saint Mary's. The reader can imagine the effect of two contiguous lakes with fifteen hundred feet difference in their levels.

It was because we wanted to see the Little Saint Mary's, only a part of which was visible from our position on Lincoln Ridge, that we resolved to climb Lincoln Peak, which lay only a short distance away at the southwestern extremity of our ridge. It was only half past eight and the horse backers had not yet left Sperry Camp (we could see all the trail to Sperry plainly); so we felt perfectly safe in making the ascent. Nor were we mistaken, for it was only a matter of half an hour's camera skinning and clothes tearing to gain the summit, from which point the view is truly remarkable. In addition to what we had seen at the ridge, one end of Lake MacDonald was plainly visible at the farthest end of Spragues Creek valley. The whole was well worth seeing despite the fact that clouds were beginning to form on Mount Jackson.

After we had remained on top some time, enjoying the beauties of the panorama but shivering before a biting wind, a grey mist so completely obscured the Mount Jackson part of the range that we hardly deemed it worth while to stay, and so returned. Our return to the trail did not prove untimely, for the equestrians of our party overtook us when we had proceeded but a short distance beyond the crest of Lincoln Ridge.

Here it becomes necessary to digress for the moment to relate a little adventure which befell our fellow traveler Miss Hyatt. At first reading, it will not appear to relate to the main narrative directly enough to warrant mention. But let me assure you, it has a definite part to play. It is not to fill space, but to show the surprising romantic influence over the individual, which is generated by mountain air. This influence is especially potent in its domination of females, as is plainly demonstrated in the present instance.

Thoroughly to appreciate the affair the reader must be informed of some of the general characteristics of mountain horses . They are generally addicted to the habit of overeating and consequently to the kindred indisposition, gas on the stomach. For this reason, it is no uncommon sight to see creatures more like balloons than young horses, waddling about with their sides sticking out so that the saddle girth can hardly be buckled.

Now it happened that Miss Hyatt's horse, when he had reported for duty after a night's feeding in Sperry valley, was invested with a miniature gas plant. Since, for this reason, her horse's saddle had not been strapped as tight as usual, it was a very natural development that the saddle should come come loose after some hour and a half's vigorous exercise on the part of the horse. The eventual moment came just as "Slicker Carrie" as going down an unusually steep place. The first warning she uttered as she found herself gliding onto the neck of her steed, was a shriek (a shriek such as is uttered by the fair maiden of the enchanted palace when she sees her rescuer balked by a dragon). Jennings was off his horse and at her side in a moment. Without waiting for ceremony Miss Hyatt cast her arms around the neck of the astonished Jennings in fond embrace, and suffered him to lift her to the ground. I have never seen a more thoroughly "Romeo and Julietish" bit of pantomime; and all because of the mountain air, I am certain, for Miss Hyatt would never have thought of such an astounding feat back in Indiana.

When se had taken lunch after reaching Lake Louise's shore, father and I began the steep ascent of Gunsight Pass (a ledge joining the Jackson and Lincoln – Gunsight Ridges just southwest of Mount Jackson) leaving the girls to follow with the horses. With female perversity, they followed us afoot, disregarding our suggestion that they come with Jennings and the horses. So our party of six (Jennings had with him a six-foot cowboy friend who was driving some light horses to Midvale) was strung out over about two miles of the trail. When the first section (father and I) was about half way up the long – menacing cloud finally opened up the flood gates with an announcing celebration of terrific lightning and thunder. We beat a hasty retreat under an overhanging ledge of rock. There we waited, watching the blue waters of the lake fade into an icy black. The thunder was fearful, for each peal blended so perfectly with the echoes that the whole valley was in a continual uproar. After a few moments of this delightful entertainment, the girls put in an appearance and joined us under the cliff. Jennings later followed suit.

Mountain storms, although furious while they last, are fortunately of no great duration during the summer months. This one lasted about three quarters of an hour, after which period of time we were able to start the final hog which brought us to the final crest of the pass.

The outlook from that point was very disappointing, for all we could see was the mere outline of Gunsight Lake, about which, around which, above which, hung absolutely impenetrable curtains of cloud. As there were no signs of clearing, we started down toward the lake somewhat disgruntled. But we soon encountered that which made us forget all else. The trail became so "interesting" that Miss Hyatt declared her intentions of dismounting, and off she came, resolved to come down "that steep place" on foot. Mother gamely stuck to the saddle, although she voiced the sentiment that we had better say goodbye to her, as she sidled down a steep snowdrift. So we proceeded – "Dutch," Jennings' friend, leading with his light horses, mother next, the two horses of Miss Hyatt and Mr. Jennings, then father, and finally Jennings and Miss Hyatt.

Down, down, down we went over a trail of varying character: each part seemed worse than the part before. Finally it became a mere ledge gouged out of a 70 degree grade of loose shale.

At this stage of the descent, "Dutch" stopped the long line of horses that Miss Hyatt might catch up with and mount her horse, for we soon would go below the timber-line, he said, where the bushes might re-wet her clothes. As Mr. Jennings and Miss Hyatt were far behind, the wait was not a short one; entirely too long from mother's point of view, for she was afraid, she admits, that the long line of close-standing horses might joggle off the cliff.

So it was that mother called to father and me, the nearest human beings, to come to her rescue. Such an action on our part would seem perfectly proper and heroic, but circumstances were by no means propitious for such gallantry. The trail, only about a foot wide, was already crowded with horses, while on either side the precipitancy of the cliff was anything bur inviting. After much slipping and sliding, father got around to her from below, and I from above. This arrangement was perfectly satisfactory to all except father, who would necessarily be the under man in case of our sudden descent over the shale rock cliff. But no such disastrous result accompanied our wait. We were all still there when Jennings came up with Miss Hyatt, so fagged that she was more dead than alive, but still able to gurgle "Grin and bear it," in feeble accents.

When once started, it took us but a few minutes to come below the timber-line onto fairly level ground. Here we once more encountered that diminutive Inferno commonly called a mountain thunder shower. The cannonading was even worse than before – so bad that it frightened our horses into a gallop. When I reached the Saint Mary's River after a wild run after father, who had mounted one of the light horses, I had my first experience at riding. (This was inevitable, for the stream is too deep and wide to pass on foot.) With the air of a tried equestrian I mounted and started across, but my horse changed his mind, and we galloped off from the rest of the party to a little parking or meadow where he kicked up his heals at the lightning for a few minutes. After this ceremony we galloped back to, and over the river. The last mentioned stunt was executed so violently that I got another rinsing, but such a trifle as a ducking had by this time become too insignificant for my notice. Once in camp, I toppled off my mount and staggered into a tent to the side of a warm stove, by the side of which I steamed until my clothes were dry, until my scattered wits and my good humor had returned, until I was cheerfully ruminating on the events of Gunsight Trip.

Chapter V

The Gunsight Pass Camp is situated at the source of the Saint Mary's River, at the northeast extremity of Gunsight Lake, in the midst of a most impressive group of mountains, Directly east of the camp rises the knob of Blackfeet Mountain, above the base of which is visible one great wing of Blackfeet Glacier. Northeast of the valley, Citadel Mountain is well situated to attract and charm the eye. The surprising feature of this mountainis that it looks too "man-ish" to be a work of nature. Its massive sides rise in regular terraces, thus uniformly diminishing the mountain's bulk until the summit assumes the aspect of an invulnerable fortress, from which some prehistoric natives might have domineered their inferiors. Fusilade Mountain forms the western boundary, and some distance to the northeast looms the block top of Going-to-the-Sun. Gunsight Camp is probably the most centrally located of any in the park with regard to mountains.

The one surprising fact about the location is that it does not command a view of Mount Jackson, the largest and nearest of all the group. But such a curious situation is not an uncommon one; nor is it difficult to explain. Just in front of the camp a massive mound of loose shale rock rises to a height apparently as great as that of Fusilade. This is the beginning of Mount Jackson's foothill ridge, which extends far back, skirting the edges of Blackfeet, Harrison, and Ellsworth Glaciers, finally terminating in the main spine of Jackson's summit. So mount Jackson is obscured from the curious eyes of tourists by one of her most insignificant foothills.

I confess I don't know whether it was the great altitude of Mount Jackson that lured us or whether it was the effeminate trait of curiosity to know what lay behind that shale mound, which made us try the ascent of Mount Jackson. At any rate we did make such a decision and on the second morning of our stay in the Gunsight vicinity, we might have been seen climbing the Blackfeet Glacier trail preparatory to ascending the mound of shale.

We were in the best of spirits, for all our earthly affairs had been so arranged tha we were free to roan about at or leisure until our thirst should be satiated. Over my shoulder was swung the trusty knapsack with its unual load of camera and lunch. The camp proprietor had very thoughtfully given us a can of beans and one of sardines, both f which were minus their openers. (He evidently felt called upon to wreak his vengeance one way if not another for being compelled to furnish us this elaborate lunch for the paltry sum of one dollar and a quarter!) The girls had gone ahead to the Narrows. The weather was as near fair as it had ever been during our sojourn in the park. Our blisters were failrly healed. The outlook was on the whole so favorable that we felt in the best of condition to tackle any variety of technical difficulty in the field of mountaineering, even though we had no guide.

It was not long until we had a chance to "try our metal." When we came to the open a short distance from the moraines of Blackfeet Glacier we decided to proceed directly up the shale mound and so save ourselves the long, out-of-the-way trip around Blackfeet. The route did prove to be a short cut in distance but not with regard to difficulty. The side of the great mound turned out to be a great pile of loose rock. Even enormous boulders weighing tons were so insecurely settled in the fine sandy shale that they were hardly safe to climb under. We were over two hours in reaching the crest of that steep treacherous mound. We were all but compelled to resort to the Irishman's expedient of walking backward, for it was almost a case of "one step up and a slide of two steps back." Such climbing is the kind the mountaineer dreads more than any other. It is not thrilling and invigorating but it is nevertheless dangerous. And climbing where the nerves as well as the muscles are on a constant tension, is the most fatiguing and discouraging.

By the time we did reach the summit of the shale mound, weather conditions had taken an alarming trun. Great black clouds had srung up everywhere, casting an ominous gloom over mountains and valley. A wind, so powerful and steady that it rendered standing upright on the ledge-summit of the mound impossible, swept our wall of rock with the fury of a legion of demons, striving to level the battlements of their Arch-enemy. The roar was so deafening that father, ten feet behind me, could not hear a word I said, even though I shouted at the top of my voice. It was like the bursting of the Bag of the Winds.

The vast stretch before us was rendered all the more appalling by the signs of the approaching storm. The bald, rocky summit of Mount Jackson, which lay some two miles distant at the top of the steep ridge on which we found ourselves, looked quite inaccessible because of a sheer wall of rock five hundred feet high, which broke the rise in the ridge some half mile from the summit. The summit was itself partially obscured by a dingy grey cloud. On the southwest side of our ridge the 80% slope of fine shale stretched some two thousand feet below us, finally losing itself in a seething chaos of black, grey, and copper-colored mist. The long, horseshoe-shaped ledge with this disorder beneath, and the pandemonium of wind above and below, might well have passed for the crater of a colossal volcano on the eve of belching forth its deadly fumes. This awful display, with the five hundred foot precipice as a background, was well calculated to shake the nerves of the best of climbers.

I looked dubiously at father and he looked dubiously at me, but we resolved to "stick it out" at least, until we should gain the base of that forbidding wall. So we proceeded into the very jaws of an elemental Hades, - now descending behind one side or other of the ridge-crest, with the enraged wind jamming us mercilessly against the rocks; now crawling timorously to the crest where the titanic drive of the blast would send us sliding back below, fearful lest we should be whisked off like two feathers into the very heart of the tempest. It was like standing on the ends of the earth and gazing into a Miltonian chaos. Our progress was slow in the face of such conditions and by dint of indiscriminate use of fingers and hobnails. We finally scrambled under some sheltering rocks at the base of Maximus Locus Praeceps, - the wall.

At this juncture, the clouds below very obligingly rolled away, and we had a momentary glance at the crevasse-scored surfaces of Blackfeet and Harrison Glaciers (four thousand feet below) on one side, and of Gunsight Lake and hanging Ellsworth Glacier on the other. Gunsight lake was a mile almost directly under us. But the glance was only momentary. Almost immediately the curtain rolled back, there to remain for the rest of the day.

Then we began to ascent of the precipice – a bit of real mountain climbing – with an especially violent wind to celebrate our start; or possibly to "get in voice," as I thought at the time, for the chanting of our funeral dirge. The wind, however, was really an advantage. Its direction was such that it served well to hold us to the rocky side in places where the attraction of gravity was powerless to fulfill this obligation. That five hundred feet of rock was the most obstinate of any that I have ever tried to mount. We made at least three starts, each one of which terminated in some impossible cliff. On the fourth attempt, the clouds so completely enveloped us that we could only see the wall in front of us and were so spared the disconcerting influence of those "over-the-shoulder" glances which are anything but pleasant when the climber is in precarious position. After much frantic scrambling and pawing of the rocks with our hobnail claws, we managed to gain traction enough to worm our way up the baffling cliff, - to pass the most forbidding obstacle of the climb. Once we were conscious of a most unusual sensation. We seemed on a floating island miles away from everything and everybody, marooned in a lonely universe of cloud. Perhaps it was better to be ignorant of our surroundings for the ridge had changed in character after the precipice and was now a wall, each side of which was perpendicular as far down as we could follow it with cloud-dimmed eyes. We learned later that the base of this wall was uncomfortably far down; so, after all, the clouds were useful to keep us in blissful ignorance. About a half an hour from the precipice top brought us to the summit, which is the highest of three adjacent knobs of the ridge.

Although the clouds were very dense about and above us, the savage wind had somewhat thinned them out below – so much so that we could look down on the tiny form of Gunsight Lake and on the pass which we had before thought so high. On the other side we could see nothing; so we gave up hope temporarily and retreated under a cave-like gulch just below the summit, to eat lunch.

Lunch! – so refreshing and renovating as a usual thing – how false did it prove here! Cheese never did charm my appetite to any great extent, and as for the bread, it had an aggravating habit of cruising off into the abyss of cloud, monoplane fashion, with every gust of wind. We went so far as to get out the cans of sardines and beans, but here we were again balked by that act of vengeance on the part of the camp proprietor. Since, for this reason we had no can openers, we gave up this part of the lunch and thrust it back into the knapsack for future use. Pickles alone were left and these we consumed ravenously. The were not so sweet as they might have been, and my face and teeth were soon respectively twisting and chattering from another cause besides the extreme cold. I fear Mr. Davidson, the camp proprietor, would not have felt particularly edified if he could have read my thoughts at that time!

After about a half an hour we started down since the clouds were becoming even heavier than before. The return trip proved to be much easier than we had expected. The first lap was of course the hardest. After descending the precipice and reaching the lowest end of the ridge, the work of the trip was over; for all that remained was the descent of the shale ridge. Although there was about two miles of this – and a very steep two miles – descent over loose shale is the best of sport. We chose a place to descend nearer the camp and much steeper than we had dared to ascend. Our course lay for the first mile and a half over this steep slope of fine, sandy shale. After this lay a broad apparently flat snowdrift. Below this stretched the shrubbery zone. Thus we outlined our return, planning to go to camp by way of the Glacier trail.

With a whoop and a yell we started down, I leading by about a hundred feet to "try" the rock and look out for "blind bluffs." (These are rock precipices ranging from fifty to a hundred feet in height which are indiscernible when looked at from above, even when but a short distance away.) It was like traveling in seven league boots, for we covered about ten feet with every stride in the sandy rock. The shale descent was like a dream all except the last part where the rocks were larger and too firm to slide.

Coming suddenly over a little hillock, I encountered the snowdrift, which descended over a half a mile in front in a 45% to 50% slope. As the snow seemed soft, I went ahead with a shout to father. The first hundred yards was truly delightful, for the cooling snow was like velvet to my feet. Then matters began to take on an interesting aspect. Without warning the snow began to change to ice on which I had little or no control of my speed. As matters grew worse I held my breath in dread apprehension. It was a fatal mistake for it lost me my balance. The next minute I was sliding along on the already overworked seat of my trousers. As this part of my outfit was not armed with hobnails my speed was decidedly increased. Giddy and breathless, I desperately thrust out my hands as last resort brakes. After being conscious for a moment of the sharp, burning pain of friction, I arrived at the bottom of the drift which, fortunately for me, flattened out before it gave place to the rocks. My descent had been so rapid that father had not noticed, for I could plainly see him high up on the drift, picking his way down as if nothing had happened. For several minutes I could do nothing but gaze at my poor hands, which were very sore and red as ripe tomatoes. It seemed incredible that I had made such a reckless slide without more serious consequences.

About an hour later, when we were quite near the camp, and had stopped to eat our can of beans, (Father had a last consented to sacrifice one blade of his pocket knife.) I was able to laugh at my adventure; but none before.

From "Bean Station" it was but a short distance to the camp, where we were only too glad to rest, and busy ourselves with our special duties: father's, to wash off his blistered pedal extremities; mine, to write up in my diary the features of the Mount Jackson climb.

Chapter VI

The night following our eventful Mount Jackson trip was bleak and gusty, with just enough fine sleet swirling around our portable tents to make the canvas roofs rustle as if a score of "gofers" were playing hide-an'-seek thereon. But all this seemed tame after the furies of Mount Jackson –so tame that I did not trouble myself to stay awake. Father was evidently of a like mind for I heard the rhythmic buzz from his cot even before I had accomplished the feat of pulling my soaked shoes off. Ours were surely "two minds with but a single thought" – the pleasure of a good night's sleep. And we enjoyed that pleasure, I am ashamed to say, until half past eight the next morning.

Mr. Jennings had told us the trail to the Narrows was only ten miles long, we did not leave until nine o'clock. Even this start was somewhat earlier than we had expected, for it had been our hope to pose for a time as the heroes of the camp after our strenuous climb of the day before. But Dame Circumstance punished our vanity: when we went to the Ram Pasture (mountain slang for sitting room tent) we found its only occupant to be Mr. Davidson, the proprietor, who was calmly pouring coal-oil into the stove to revive the dying fire. Mr. Davidson, the coal-oil can, and the stove were hardly an inviting reception committee, especially when the last two members were so close together. Under the circumstances father paid the bill rather hastily and with even more consternation than he usually shows on such occasions.

Once more we fell into our hiking stride as we followed the horse-tracks to the Narrows. We both were quite jubilant as we plunged into the forest, for the path was broad, the horse-tracks unmistakable, and Jenning's map fairly lucid. The path lay through broken pine forest. One minute our feet would crunch on a matting of pine needles as we threaded our way among tapering trees. The next, we would thump over soft grassy parklands, studded with a variety of wild flowers (especially the fiery Indian Paintbrush). These parklands are very common throughout the park. They are the sites, so Jennings says, of the snow lakes that form in the spring when the mountains are getting rid of their winter finery. This fact probably accounts for the profusion of flowers in such places later in the year. The flowers I shall ever recall as the most charming part of the tramp from Gunsight to the Narrows.

About a half an hour later after we had plunged into unbroken forest, we encountered a caravan of three men and eight horses. Each horse had some four or five long boards chained behind him and the eight animals proceeded in single file with about twenty feet between each one. You can readily see how three men would be kept busy with such a charge when you remember how crooked mountain trails are. It takes considerable ingenuity to get the longer boards around the sharp curves, and someone is giving orders most of the time. Long after they had passed us we could hear the regular fall of feet, the shouting of the men and the scraping of the boards. I have mentioned the incident because it typifies the crudeness of the place. It can be realized what a colossal task it is to build hotels in this region when every board must be hauled in this manner.

A sharp turn of the trail brought us suddenly to a marshy clearing through which meandered the Saint Mary's River. To our left rose heavily-wooded bluffs, but to the right we could command a longed-for panorama. Through the long slender reeds of the marshland we could plainly perceive a great bald-headed peak which could be no other than Mount Jackson. This was our first view of the mountain we had climbed. When on Gunsight Pass, we had lost old Jackson in a cloud. Then on its very sides we had but momentary views of it. Now it loomed up against an azure sky, with a tiny white cloud near its summit – an aerial counterpart of Ellsworth Glacier. It was not until the camera had clicked several times that we discovered a beautiful mountain some distance to the right of Mount Jackson. It was Fusilade, but not the Fusilade we had known at Gunsight. Then, it had looked like a long barricade, but now it stood out against its azure background, in form a veritable Matterhorn. This apparent change in aspect of the mountain is due to its shape. It is similar in form to a section of jagged track-rail: when viewed from the front, it is broad; when viewed from the end, sharp and narrow. Midway between the two mountains was a tiny notch in the ridge. My first glance at this notch reminded me of my Colt Automatic Pistol sight. A moment later I accounted for the idea. We were undoubtedly gazing at Gunsight Pass. For the first time the significance of the name fully impressed me. The camera of course clicked once more and the result is the beautiful picture which now adorns our parlor. Would that my meager capital would permit of a reproduction of the picture in these pages! Alas, it cannot be, my dear reader. There is unfortunately a limit to possibility and I have rashly trod on the border land. Pray let my blunder pass.

From this beautiful panorama we turned reluctantly away and followed the uninviting path as it lead a gradual but steady ascent through ever deepening forest. My one consoling thought was that every step would bring us nearer the gigantic cube, Going-to-the-Sun, which we had been steadily approaching, although the forest cut off all possibilities of a view. By degrees my spirits began to ebb, and I sought the solace of a cake of Hershey's Milk Chocolate. Father uttered no word of complaint, but I could not help noticing that he had ceased to comment on the grandeur of the forest, and he seemed more concerned about horse-tracks than tree-foliage. At this crisis Dame Circumstance again took a hand, but it was feeble encouragement that she brought. I suddenly discovered a dingy bit of paper carefully folded and stuck on a branch beside the trail. Upon opening it I beheld the following inscription:

"Jimmy was a hiker, long un' lank un' lean,

Uh – uh –uh - uh –uh - uh –uh - uh –uh - uh –uh,

He was ever teasing for some eats an' bean,

Uh – uh –uh - uh –uh – um."

This outburst of poetic feeling was evidently genuine and without doubt the work of the Chaminade rival (for the regular "uh's" probably indicated a musical interlude to heighten the excellence of this ditty.) But there was not enough encouragement in the verses to counteract our spell of the grouch. To make matters worse, I happened to gaze at my pedometer and my watch. The watch said twelve o'clock and the pedometer eight miles. The fear kept haunting me that we might not get to the Narrows until the dining tent had closed. The thought of such a calamity was most harrowing.

But the Fates were only darkening our way that we should enjoy even more the sight they had prepared for us. After twenty minutes of dismal uphill climbing we emerged, without warning, on the crest of a bare knoll of rock. Before us – nay rather, above us – lowered the entire bulk of Going-to-the-Sun. We beheld the great mount with no petty foothill to obstruct our view. In truth, the mountain has no foothills that are adjacent to its base. It rises like one great block from the almost level plateau immediately surrounding it. It is not a solid block as I had at first thought. On the west side near the summit there is a hollow which is perpetually filled with snow. The grand old mountain bears the semblance of an altar with its sheer sides and the hollowed-out summit ready for the offering. Perhaps the Indians had that resemblance in mind when they gave to it the impressive name, Going-to-the-Sun. Who knows? The possibility is too great to be sneered at. They may well have deemed the great block the altar on which the elements make their sacrifices to the Great Spirit. Surely no sanctuary could be more becoming the dignity and might of the Great Spirit!

After all, these Indian folk had an admirable respect for nature. They surely saw and appreciated the presence of deity in these great natural monuments. Where Indian nomenclature remains, it in itself expresses their attitude of reverence. Gong-to-the-Sun, Heaven's Peak: - what white explorers would have given such names? It is one of the failings of the white man to name after himself every natural wonder which he, by mere caprice of Fate, discovers. If Jones discovers a mountain, you may rest assured it will be Jones' Peak or else the creek at its base will be Jones' River. Somewhere in the neighborhood you will find the name Jones. I do not insinuate that such action is crime; but merely egotism - an egotism not to be found in the red man's character. The Indians may have been superstitious, but withal they were religiously humble. They coupled such things as these mountains not with their own insignificant kind, but with their conception of the Great Spirit. They have lent a dignity to Glacier Park that has lived after them and will continue to live. Ours is a debt of gratitude.

My stomach was the guilty agent that finally awoke me from my Going-to-the-Sun reverie. The spirit can soar just so high on an empty stomach and then the dreamer is reminded that his existence is still corporal. So it was with me. That internal gnawing finally reminded me to look in the direction of our goal. - O terque beata visio!! There, not more than two miles distant, lay the beautiful waters of the Saint Mary's River and the Upper Lake Saint Mary. There, too, were the rough boarded tops of the chalets. Father seems quite as much impressed by this new feature of the landscape as I; so we immediately started to follow the path farther.

But starting is as far as we got. The trail seemed to have lost itself on the top of the knolls and the horse-tracks were no longer visible because of the rockiness of the ground. Since there were two directions taken by the blazed trees we decided on the process of elimination for finding our way. The first trail led us, after some detouring, to the edge of the lake where it abruptly stopped. The builder of this thoroughfare evidently expected the tourist to fly or swim the remainder of the journey to the chalets, which were plainly visible about a mile and a half beyond, across a small gulf of the lake. Since we were not in a mood for either experiment and since the shoreline appeared too dense to follow, we scram bitterly back to our knoll, conscious of our first blunder in trail choosing.

We had followed the second trail some half hour and I began to think we were making our second blunder. Our way followed the top of a series of abrupt terraces, immediately opposite which lay the hill on which the chalets were so comfortably settled. To our consternation, the trail, instead of leading down the terraces, kept mounting higher and higher, farther and farther from our goal. Finally I suggested that we try our hand at getting down from these terraces "sine via." This course was not inviting, however, for we had no idea when we might strike an impassible precipice in the terraces. Then, too, the forest beneath looked formidable. As we paused in hesitation the clang of dinner gong pleaded cheerfully at the chalets. The suggestion came at the psychological moment and we both rushed toward the terrace edges, resolved to take a chance at the forest and gully.

The beginning or our descent was encouraging. The first terrace was about fifty feet in height, but ridges in the rock made our descent a matter of little difficulty. But then came trouble – in the form of a jump-off not much deeper than the first, but absolutely perpendicular. We were "stumped." The wind in the mountains laughed derisively behind us and the very waters in the nearby lake rippled in mocking giggles. Then, for the first time, did I realize how Tantalus must feel when he reaches after those Tartarian grapes. We could not help laughing despite our fatigue and despair. The very inconsistency of our situation made it ludicrous. Here we were, two practiced mountaineers, balked by a mere fifty feet of rock when we were in hailing distance of our destination, within smelling distance of our dinner! Only one course now lay open to us – to follow the baffling cliff crest in hope of finding a place where we might get down. Reluctantly we stumbled along till we found such a place. With the recklessness of exhaustion, I plunged over; not even ascertaining what kind of ground was at the bottom.

Father was at my heels and together we rushed into the unknown. My first glance seemed to reveal a tree as my landing place. With frantic feet I clawed at the cliff side as it whizzed by, but all to no avail. The force of gravity had me in its clutches, and it is no respecter of persons. Finally, with great crackling of branches I struck the tree-like bush and rattled and rattled on down to terra firma. The "come-down" was novel and altogether enjoyable when I had once made sure it was a bush, not a hundred foot pine tree on which I had dropped. Father followed me but with much more grace than I had shown. In fact he did not even lose his equilibrium once during the ordeal.

As we struggled through the dense under-brush, matters became more and more interesting. The brush became so matted that our only progress was made when we condescended to crawl. Once I had started to give a word of encouragement to father, but a whip like branch gave my mouth such a whack that I was necessarily speechless. I shall always insist that this incident has had much to do with the abnormal size of my mouth; but, unfortunately for my friends, the efficiency of this organ, its power of speech, was in no way restricted, at this time. Just as my jaw was beginning to feel natural, we encountered the gully, a tiny creek, just across from which rose another wall of rock, quite as formidable as the one we had just descended. The creek only meant four wet feet, but the cliff had torn a souvenir off my coat and a slit in my trousers before I mastered it. Father fared some better with regard to clothes, but his camera was the sufferer. By the time he joined me on top, it had been totally stripped of decorations on one side. But what did we care for such trivial things as cameras? Dinner was the goal for which we raced!

Once on top of the cliff, we soon discovered the trail we had lost, and anon were in the camp. Several tenderfeet, well equipped with tramping paraphernalia, gazed in humble admiration at our tattered rags, but we were too wise to tempt circumstance a second time by trying to show off. Instead we meekly sought the entrance of the dining chalet. Here a grizzled mountaineer who called himself "Henry" met us with a gruff but hearty welcome. He was a heavy-set individual, tall of stature, queer of feature. Above the beard that covered most of his face were two little eyes, one of which surveyed us with interest while the other looked knowingly at Going-to-the-Sun. This fellow, with all his eccentricity, understood the wants of trampers. Without a word of formality he led us to a table steaming with the canned luxuries of the park; nor did he ask one question until a good dinner had braced us for the interview.

And what a dinner it was! Corn, peas, biscuits, ham, and – BEANS – VAN CAMP'S PORK AND BEANS. I have often been prone to condemn this product of Indianapolis, but I hereby swear "perdis immortals" never to take the name of BEAN in vain again. The way they spiced our trip from Gunsight to the Narrows will always make me respect this Hoosier ambrosia.

THE ASCENT OF EAGLE'S PEAK OF THE TATOOSH RANGE WASHINGTON

June 1913

Before undertaking a climb, the experienced mountaineer regards but three conditions: that of himself, the weather, and the mountain. During our sojourn in Rainier National Park two of these conditions were decidedly against us. Mountains and weather were so menacing that we were forced to be content with making the attempt to scale Eagle's Peak of the Tatoosh Range. Mount Rainier was out of the question, since its summit was constantly wrapped in snow-bearing clouds. Hence our first climbing in this government reserve was on Eagles Peak.

On the morning we had reserved for making this rock climb, we were in excellent shape, but the weather and the mountain were very threatening. In his first great discourse on "Nature," Emerson makes the statement in somewhat different wording, that Nature, in her varying moods, is a mirror in which the vicissitudes of human nature are reflected. If Mr. Emerson could have seen our Eagles Peak morning, he would surely have declared that all the masked hypocrisy and subtle fury of a Louis XI were imaged in the ever-changing sky and the mocking sun beams that would occasionally break the gloom with false promises of fair weather. The elements were unquestionably smiling villains; their deception was too evident, too gross to pass unnoticed.

The mountain was hardly attractive with its head hopelessly lost in cloud and even its base screened now and then with fleeting mists. Then, too, there were unpleasant rumors afloat among the hotel occupants to the effect that the Eagle's Peak trail was partially obliterated by snow, and that a hanging cornice made the final stretch around the precipice impassable. But such tales are not uncommon among garrulous hotel proprietors with a love for magnifying mountain climbing perils; so father and I followed our usual rule and swallowed them with a considerable amount of salt.

Soon after breakfast we purchased a lunch and started up the muddy trail, trusting our own good condition to overcome the obstacles of weather and mountain.

After and hour or more of singularly uneventful climbing, we lost the trail in a vast snow field which overspread the steep, wooded slope as far as eye could reach. Although it ranged in depth from six to fifteen or twenty feet, it was frozen hard, and we therefore ventured to proceed in the track indicated by the tree blazes. As we penetrated farther and farther into the heights of the evergreen forest, the snow became deeper and deeper and the trees more stunted and shrub-like. Occasionally we would emerge into wind-swept hollows in which the scanty trees that did exist were completely covered with drifted snow. Much back tracking and tiresome processes of elimination in finding the blaze-marked trees would be the inevitable result. As we came forth to the final clearing on the vast snow fields, it was largely a matter of guess work to ascertain the general location of the peak itself. Behind stretched only the dazzling white, checkered here and there with pines in the foreground, and completely obscured farther back; ahead, only the faint suggestion of a bluff beyond the end of the snow.

Toward this we blindly directed our way, penetrating the fickle mists and ever and anon stopping for the clouds to reveal again our bluff. Once at the base of this cliff we left the snow and ascended a very steep chimney of a very treacherous kind of mountain moss. At about twelve o'clock we scrambled over the crest of the great chimney and found ourselves on a ledge some fifty feet in width.

Directly in front of our ledge and several thousand feet below lay the Nisqually River Valley and Paradise Valley. Though the grand old summit of Mount Rainier was not visible because of the heavy clouds, the sharp pinnacle of rock known as Eagle's Peak loomed before us not two hundred feet away, at the left hand extremity of our ridge. The summit of this crag was estimated to be some two hundred feet above the ledge; so we decided to eat our lunch before undertaking this last short lap of our climb, which, from appearances, gave promise of being the most thrilling. With this plan decided on we sought a sheltering group of pine trees on the ridge and there enjoyed for about half an hour, such climber's luxuries as sardines, cheese, and cookies.

When the last of our lunch was disposed of, we carefully threw our sardines boxes into a precarious position on the precipice brink. Father was mischievous enough to crawl to the edge of the hanging drift and there, while he clung safely with his arms, to imprint steps with his free right foot right on down beyond the crest of the snow. The climbers who made the ascent of Eagle's Peak next after us must surely have had an inflated idea of our daring! Or perhaps they may have believed themselves the discoverers of the track of some marvelous monopeded mountain goat with his one pedal extremity like the right foot of a man.

After thus celebrating our sojourn on the ridge, we immediately plunged into a wild, closely-grown thicket of evergreens which separated us from the bluff. My vague recollection of penetrating that barrier of living green is hardly pleasant, for I had to take a thorough whipping in the course of the trip. The branches, evidently seeing that my hands were both occupied in carrying a camera, a tripod and a sigma chi poster, smote me gleefully, quite well aware that I was more defenseless than Father, who had gone ahead with the ice ax. Finally I stumbled blindly against the wall and stopped to free my battered visage of the pine needle decoration. When my eyes were once more in working order we began to plan our course up the cliff.

There appeared to be a trail at the very base of the cliff, which skirted the corrugated wall. Since this "trail" lost itself in a hanging cornice at one extremity, we hastily sought the other end, which was a three thousand vertical drop. For several moments I was, I confess, sick with horror to see father contemplating a diagonal crawl out over the very chasm itself; but, though he is fearless as a mountain goat, he has a Switzer's shrewdness and so he abandoned the project when the ice ax revealed the uncertain stratification of the rock. Only one course lay open since there were no convenient chimneys in the rock, and that was a direct ascent of the cliff. On this plan of attack we proceeded to act.

After three unsuccessful attempts, father with his Switzer intuition found the one route (and I believe the **only** route) over which any human being, no matter how skilled, could have climbed. When I had watched father worm his way up the cliff, I deposited my luggage and followed with but little difficulty, for when my feet could find no hold and dangled useless, my sharp fingers and long, "ape-arms" served me faithfully. After about eight minutes on the precipice we scrambled over the crest and on to the pinnacled summit.

Though one glance reveled to us that we must forego the privilege of seeing Rainier, we were awed and in a measure satisfied by the wild chaos of seething cloud which masked our summit. In fact Father was actually moved to compose some poetry of sickly meaning but sound meter, and I followed suit with an even more unhealthy specimen of verse. These two effusions we ceremoniously sealed in an olive bottle. Then we returned to the precipice, feeling that we had duly saluted the mountain (which would have been justified in falling down on us after our desecration of its crest.)

Father preceded me in descending the cliff and gained a position beyond the evergreen thicket, so that he might get a picture of me while still in the act of descent. It was after the taking of this picture that I had the experience which keeps memories of Eagles's Peak fresh in my mind. I necessarily descended so slowly while on the precipice that Father was well beyond the lunch ridge when I hastily collected my camera outfit at the base of the cliff and penetrated the thicket. After a few minutes of the awkward progress which marked my previous trip through the tangle, I was happily surprised to find what appeared to be a trail. I followed it rapidly, soon coming to the opening at the head of our familiar chimney; but to my amazement, Father was nowhere in sight. I shouted and was bewildered to hear an answer not below me but around a pendant shoulder of the rock to get my bearings. I shouted again and my own voice mocked me in my predicament with a roar of echo. A moment later came Father's shout, fainter than before, but audible still, around the promontory. He was looking for me but in the wrong direction! The horrifying realization of what the sprite Echo can do made me shudder and I quickened my pace as I started around the shoulder, about twenty feet above where the rock terrace met the steep snow field which stretched some two hundred feet below to the front of the precipice of Eagle's Peak.

Then that most dreaded of occurrences flashed the tension of terror through me – a cave-in: just an insignificant landslip, but quite enough of a one to tilt me over backward. After a terrific moment of bumping and sliding over the great terrace I dropped a score of feet on to the steep snow slide. With a swerve like a skidding toboggan, I whizzed helplessly down toward the fatal goal, my steel hobnails scoring useless grooves on the bluish crust. It was soon to be a matter of life and death I realized, as the two hundred feet became one hundred, then fifty; so I let go both camera and poster as I swung myself forward with the force of frenzy and thrust the sharp tripod, point first, into the frozen crust. In it went, and in I went, clear to the shoulders, a human peg thrust headfirst into the drift. Before moving, I said a prayer of thanksgiving that I was not in the plight of the camera. Plainly could I hear it above the roaring in my ears: thump – thump – thump; - then silence, as it dropped over the terrific front precipice. It would fall over half a mile before hitting again! Three thousand feet below my camera would become but a shattered mass of glass, shutter, and box! I had learned my lesson: never again would I climb without both hands free. When the first paralysis of panic left me, I backed out of my hole in the snow, shook myself free of the packed slush that filled hair, mouth, sleeves, and leggings. Then I crawled on around, far below the rock shoulder. Once by the promontory, I beheld Father, a mere speck on the far end of our familiar chimney. After much yelling and hurrying I reached him and heaved my first sigh of relief.

We discussed the situation with regard to the camera, and, as we trudged back to the hotel over the less strenuous snow fields, decided to buy a duplicate of the lost camera (which belonged to my father's sister) and "hush up" the affair. This policy we adopted, and my fall is still a matter unknown to Mother and Miss Ida. M. Andrus, our traveling companions. My most thrilling adventure will thus remain hidden in silence until those two peruse these lines or Aunt Carrie's sharp eyes perceive several minor details of difference between the new and the old camera. Tum felis e crumena!!!

THE CLIMB OF MOUNT TEMPLE , CANADIAN ROCKIES

July 6, 1913

The wild jangling of an alarm bell clattered harshly through my dark surroundings and I realized for the moment what a fear-inspiring combination strange noises and opaque darkness are. Then, as the paralysis of nightmare began to leave my senses, the sound of that bell softened until I came to the ridiculous realization, when fully awake, that it was the tinkle of our telephone. The night clerk of the Lake Louise Chateau was giving us a needed reminder (at two o'clock in the morning) that the time for beginning the climb of Mount Temple was at hand.

Father had evidently been awake when the ring came, for I saw him gazing out of the window before I had entirely collected my wits. For several seconds I waited in dread apprehension, but when the night-shirted spectre at the window did speak, he uttered that longed-for word, fair. Animated as if by an electric vitalizer, I immediately started to climb into my climber's "glad rags" consisting of rawhide shoes (decorated outside by murderous hobnails and inside by a clammy fresco of green mould), canvas leggings, a faded negligee shirt, and the skeleton of a brown suit. Though donning damp clothes is a slow task, Father and I negotiated it in fairly short order, and fifteen minutes after the telephone's outburst we were crunching down the dark corridors of the hotel in a vain effort to walk on hob-nailed tiptoes.

Once in the atrium, we were piloted by the night-watchman to a breakfast awaiting us in the side wing of the dining room. At two in the morning, a breakfast of cold ham, tomatoes, cucumbers, onions, and pie is hardly appetizing, but Father and I ate from a sense of duty, for plenty of food is the climber's safe guard against weakness and vertigo.

After breakfast we sought the side court of the Chateau where we were joined in a few moments by Mr. Achen, our fellow-climber from

New York, and later by Rudolf (our Switzer), and four horses. The task of distributing baggage was difficult in the uncertain light of the first dawning gray splotches in the sky. Finally, the huge rucksack was tight behind the saddle of our stalwart Switzer. Then, with a flourish of ice axes, we trotted down the gully through which runs the Paradise Valley Road. Soon the Chateau and all its environment was lost in the purple, translucent mists of first morning rays. We were alone with Nature. We were on our way to climb the greatest old peak in Alberta's goodly host of Canadian Rockies. That was all I felt, all I cared.

In the mountain landscape a few hours before sunrise, there is more perfect harmony of beauty than at any other time. One trip at this time of day over the Paradise Valley Road would be enough to convince the most persistent skeptic, I am sure. There is a murky sweetness of odour to the trees and a soft delicacy of outline to the stately pines never perceptible at any other season of t the day. The fringy fingers of' the spruce are more exquisite than ever, for the absence of wind makes each branch and twig sharply outlined. The absolute stillness makes visible, too, the dainty lacework of evergreen that hangs web like on the drooping branches of the cedar. Far beyond, through the network of green, the grander beauty of the mountains is apparent. Then are they not mundane beeps of carefully studied rock and charted glaciers. They temporarily lose that exactness of dimension and become like Dore's mountains, mystic and fairy- like in their vastness and depth of color. You may laugh at and contemn me as a dreamer, but I tell you even the most intensely scientific of individuals must lose his analytic attitude under such circumstances. There is an irresistible psychic appeal to the imagination which baffles analysis. One must feel it to understand it.

About four miles of riding in the open road brought us to the parting of the Paradise Valley Trail and the Ten Peaks Valley Road. After some ten minutes' trot on the former, we came to a parking which commanded an awe- inspiring view of Mount Temple. From that time on, our trail kept repeatedly returning to the

open; so, as we skirted the northwest base of Mount Temple, we had ample opportunity to observe the beautiful ridge or valley rim connecting Pinnacle Peak, Eiffel Crags, and Mount Hungabee; also three sides of Mount Temple itself, the monarch of the region, were visible.

Mount Temple stands alone and so possesses a peculiar grandeur. Unlike Mount Sir Donald, it has no pinnacled peak of rock, but, instead, a great glacial summit of ice and snow. Rudolf Aemmer, our Swiss guide, informed us that sections of the snow neve which banks up to form the corniced mountain summit, are over one hundred and fifty feet deep. At its lower extremity, this glistening snow field deepens from white to pale blue, where the glacier ice begins to show through its covering, since Mount Temple is block-like in shape, much like Going to-the-Sun Mountain in Glacier National Park, snow can bank itself only very high up on the on the top of the block: hence the mighty glaciers at an altitude above eleven thousand feet.

At about half pasted six we reached a camping hollow in the basin of the great Citadel-Eiffel-Hungabee Ridge. Here we left the horses and with ice axes, rope, and rucksack, started up Sentinel Pass, having first ascertained that our saddles were safely hung in trees out of reach of curious porcupines. The trail led steadily up a gradual ascent toward a cut between Mount Temple arid Citadel Mountain. This cut is wall-shaped and backed up with fine, loose shale rocks. For two hours we zigzagged our way over this uncertain Pass. The one compensation for the difficult and dangerous rock climbing was the fact that we passed almost under the peak and the phantastic side crags of Citadel. Of these side crags one is particularly noticeable. It is hardly fifty feet in diameter, but it towers several hundred feet above its slender base, tilting from Citadel at such a great angle that it sends a long sable shadow far over the white snow fields of Sentinel Pass. I could hardly suppress a shudder as we, mere human beings, crawled under this crazy shaft, which seemed but waiting to get a good chance to thunder down on us. Mr. Achen must have had some similar misgiving, for while we picked our way through the shadow, he gazed up several times and puffed smothered exclamations from his over—worked wind pipe.

But Deus Montanus was with us, and at eight thirty we had safely passed the menacing shadows and were on the crest of Sentinel, Pass. Here we had our second breakfast and stretched our snow-dampened feet in the warm sunlight.

The Ten Peaks, as they burst upon us from Sentinel Pass, have made an indelible impression on my memory note book. The moment we gained the Pass their ridge became visible—a great snow—checkered wall lifting its ten distinct summits almost a mile above the snowy plateau known as the Valley of the Ten Peaks. Preeminent among these peaks is a great triangular mass of ice and rock, well named Deltaform. Though three hundred feet lower than Mount Temple it is a terrific climb. In fact, it has only been climbed twice, and in those instances the mountaineers were on its treacherous cliffs for twenty-seven hours. It well deserves to be lord of the Ten Peaks. So we unanimously agreed as Rudolf buckled on the rucksack and we left the Pass for the rocky side of Temple itself.

For an hour or more, our main difficulty consisted in mounting a seventy per cent shale slope. This climbing was indeed a thorough workout - somewhat in the nature of an initiation for our friend Achen, who had never before climbed above the lower altitudes where the breath is not a factor to be reckoned with.

Finally the loose shale gave place to ever enlarging terraces; so, under a convenient bluff of red quartz rock, we roped up ad proceeded with all the caution that such climbing requires. From this point of roping up to the next lunch stop was the most thrilling part of the climb. A few moments after leaving the rock terrace of red quartz, Rudolf led the way up an ever narrowing gulch in the great cliffs until we found ourselves knee deep in the snow of a great "chimney" drift. (A chimney is a narrow defile in a sheer precipice, either the result of erosion or strata-slips. It is the old standby of the climber, for it renders climbing possible in otherwise inaccessible places. Up this near-wall we crunched, taking care to keep in Rudolf's tracks. There is nothing like a chimney drift to make one cautious and observant of the every word of one's guide. Once over the crest, we beheld ahead of us, at the farther end or a gradual snow slope, a great castle—like series of quartz rocks, similar to, but more massive than the ones we had before climbed over. Toward this wall we went, eventually skirting its base. After some little climbing (as near the rock as the cornices of our snow drift would permit) we ascended a second chimney and emerged on a flat hollow on the cliff where we prepared and greedily devoured our first lunch.

The panorama which our secluded hollow commanded gave most striking evidence of the metamorphosis which all objects seem to undergo when viewed from a great elevation. The imposing line of the Ten Peaks no longer formed a wall to obscure our view but rather a mere rim to the Ten Peaks Plateau, beyond which in- numerable mountains loomed up in sharp relief. We were, in fact, on a level with all the summits of the Ten Peaks except that of Deltaform which still overtopped us, but by little more than three hundred feet. There is a particu1ar point on the side of every high mountain, from which the climber can command a very curious view of his surroundings. From such a point the surrounding mountains still retain some of the appearances which make them noteworthy to the low-land observer, but in the main they become dwarfed and flattened out like the models on a relief map. It was at this particular changing point that our lunch camp happened to be located. Thus we enjoyed all during our meager lunch hour the unusual sensation of seeing things from the half-man, ha1f-mountain goat stand-point.

At. half past eleven we again started, this time on the summit lap of our climb. Five minutes of scrambling brought us to the ridge crest of the crags, on the side of which we had eaten our lunch. Here, with all the fury of a frenzied animal there struck us one of those highland gales peculiar to altitudes greater than eleven thousand feet. From that point on, we crunched gradually up the steep but uniform slope of pure white snow ridge, ever battling to keep from soaring off on the wings of the blast. Though baffled in its attempt to unfix us, the wind at least had the satisfaction of collecting tax from us, for it whisked off Father's headgear with such violence that it was soon lost to sight as it flew over the side of the snow—corniced precipice over— hanging Paradise Valley at a height of eight thousand feet.

At about one o'clock our little quartet gained the very crest of the gigantic snow cornice which forms the highest summit of Temple. For several moments we stood upright and silent in the face of the terrific wind, as Father, Rudolf, and I drank in the view, and Mr. Achen collected his shattered nerves after a fit of mountain sickness.

Seldom can human eyes survey the stretch the stupefying sweep of' country that ours did then. For a radius of' over a hundred and fifty miles in all directions were the snow capped highlands visible, until the bright snow of the more distant summits became lost in the dazzling gray of translucent clouds. To the north-west, Mount Lefroy, Mount Sir Donald, Mount Victoria, Mount Aberdeen, Mount Sanford, and Mount Hungabee held the most noticeable positions; to the south, Mt. Deltaform and Mt. Fay of the Ten Peaks, and the more distant Mt. Assynboine. Directly north of our summit lay the phantasticly corniced snow and ice peaks of lower Temple. These distorted heeps of ice demand the respect of the climber, for they are quite inaccessible. They cannot be reached from above because of an impassable ice bank, nor from below because of over a mile of sheer rock.

But why attempt the description of such a scene? Though I detail with the utmost accuracy all the phases of the grand prospect, you cannot—alas, that it is true!—visualize my descriptions unless you have yourself tasted of the magic of high altitudes! To you, I must make the same confession that I have so frequently made to those who seek to know what pleasure Father and I find in (as they say) risking our bones on the lonely heights. There is an influence besides the mere exhilaration of physical exercise or the witnessing of grand panoramas with which the climber is blessed. For lack of a better name I call it the spirit of the Mountains. I realize how fruitless must be the task of analyzing it; so I will not attempt a work at which real authors have failed. Instead let me exhort you to become acquainted with the high mountains; not their valleys nor plateaus, but the peaks and summits themselves. When once you have known the Spirit, you will remember these apparent1y lifeless lines and they will assume new meaning.

Our descent was uneventful except for our lightning trip down Sentinel Pass . The reader will remember my description of Sentinel Pass as a wall, heaped up with fine loose shale around which we skirted in making the ascent. In going down we kept to the middle of the loose shale as we took downward strides which created miniature avalanches in themselves. Half way down the Pass we encountered a steep and lengthy Snow drift over which we tobogganed, controlling our speed by the rear pressure of our ice axes. From the base of this drift on to camp was a long but gradual descent.

When once we reached the camp the only difficulty remaining was the rounding up of our horses. This was no mean task, however, for the ambitious "caeyusas" had conceived the idea of exploring our stopping place and were at the far end of the valley when we reached camp. It was only after much puffing on the part of Rudolf that they were persuaded to desert their grassy banquet and carry us back to the Chateau over the last and most uninteresting stretch of the climb.

Thus terminated the first experience of the Wynns in genuine snow climbing, where snow chimneys and ice cornices are the order of ascent. Nothing more can we wish than such good luck in the climbs to follow!

A SHORT BIOGRAPHY OF TOPSEY WYNN

Before starting in on this sketch, it is fitting that a few words be said in explanation of the rambling style of discourse which has been employed throughout. When detailing episodes from the life of such a fickle creature as Topsey, it is well nigh, if not altogether impossible to unify her biography. Like the dog days of her life, the elements of this article must be somewhat incongruous. Trusting that this introduction may justify the singular rhetorical construction of parts of the sketch, I shall proceed without further delay to chronicle some of' the events in the life of this illustrious canine.

While the Wynnses were living at 1119 North Alabama Street, Topsey began her "cursus honoris"(at least, from a dog's point of view) by arriving one morning on the front porch, quit as if she had been thrown there with the morning paper. Consequently, when Dr. Wynn and James, the young harum-scarum, came out to get the paper, here was a skinny little black pup, all a wiggle with enthusiasm, to meet them. She immediately showed herself to he endowed with feminine astuteness, for she presented her most favorable credential first by sitting down and thrusting her little black mittens into the outstretcjec1 hands of' the young harum-scarum. This feat, deftly performed at the psychological moment, won her way to favor with the Wynnses, and she was formally adopted into the Wynn family an'-l christened Topsey because of' the dusky color of her hair and the fact that she seemed to have "just grown" off the front porch during the night. Thus, through the exercise of distinctly feminine tact, Topsey gained her place of importance in, the Wynn family.

Although possessed of a maiden's shrewdness, Topsey clearly was invested with at least one trait of maidenly folly a1so,——-a fondness for brass buttons or their wearers. So it was that she became completely infatuated, with the postman——-it was almost a case of love at first sight.

And by so doing she caused the young harum-scarum one of the most sorrowful afternoons of its life. He was first apprised of Topsey's infatuation as he was coming up Delaware Street on his way home from school. Suddenly a familiar patter of feet caused him to raise his eyes in alarm. Yes it was Topsey; and over a mile from home She bestowed a passing glance of recognition upon him and then, despite his entreaties and threats, she haughtily tossed her little black head and dashed off after the postman who was a half a block or so clown the street. Quite over—whelmed with grief and rage, the young harum-scarum paced the streets the remainder of the afternoon in a vain endeavor to ascertain the whereabouts of his wayward puppy. Meeting with no success, he finally turned his footsteps toward home where he found the exasperating Topsey waiting for him. She had followed. the postman to where he had boarded a Pennsylvania Street car, as the harum-scarum learned later, and then evidently taken a devious route home. The harum-scarum was too delighted to scold her, and so the misdemeanor was overlooked although it had caused the young master no end of worry.

The only other circumstance that has ever caused Topsey to desert her family is the Fourth of July on which occasion she invariably absconds that her delicate feelings may not have a chance to receive a jolt at the hands of some impolite cannon cracker.

After the first excitement of Topsey's arrival had subsided, the members of the Wynn family, with characteristic curiosity, began to puzzle themselves about her ancestry, but as all conjectures could only be suppositional, they finally gave up the investigation and were content to class her as plain dog of tie water spaniel type with perhaps an infinitesimal quantity of patrician blue blood in her veins. In order to ascertain whether Topsey was at all inclined toward aquatics, the young harum-scarum finally arranged an afternoon at Fall Creek during which Topsey greatly edified her reputation as a water spaniel . At two o'clock that afternoon, Dr. Wynn drove up to the house where Topsey and her master awaited him. After due amount of persuasion and help from her master, Topsey, who had picked up in flesh wonderfully since her arrival at the Wynnse managed to land in the little back balcony of the phaeton after a very unbecoming climb—scramble_jurnp,1en the little phaeton was well on its way to the creek, Topsey regained her equilibrium and self-poise enough to hark imperiously at little fox terriers and the other canaille of the wayside; in fact she became so thoroughly conscious of her social superiority that she quite forgot the necessity of maintaining her balance during her orations to the plebeians of the street, and was consequently precipitated with considerable violence from her lofty seat into the very midst of a crowd of her inferiors who lustily barked their approval of Topsey's graphic portrayal of the adage "pride goeth before a fall." Only stopping for a moment of self-inspection after her fall, chagrinned Topsey scrambled along after the phaeton, continuing her journey to the creek in a manner ill becoming her dignity. But once at the creek, she soon drowned her embarrassment in its cooling waters. Her first attempt at swimming was indeed ludicrous. Although she was successful in keeping her head partially above the surface, she caused such a disturbance in the water that waves were continually washing over her black head. Though this water agitation was somewhat disconcerting to Topsey, it was a source of even greater mischief to the young harum-scarum who was also endeavoring to learn to swim; for every time he took his feet off the bottom and began the necessary motions, Topsey deemed it essential to go to his assistance, - and go she would, with such an upheaval of water on all sides of her that the young harum-scarum would be invariably swamped with waves, would go bubbling to the bottom to emerging a moment later in anything but a pleasant state of mind. But Topsey, blissfully ignorant of his paddle along so innocently that he would immediately pardon her. After an hour or so of practice, Topsey began to minimize the splashing and to increase the efficiency of her submarine sources of propulsion so that before that afternoon was over, she was paddling the quiet stroke of a master Swimmer. Thorough1y satisfied with her progress, Dr. Wynn and the harum-scarum at last persuaded her to resume her scat in the balcony in which she road home, hot and wet, but more than ever aware of her preeminence in the dog world. Thereafter, Topsey has always been considered a water spaniel of the most aquatic of temperaments.

Sometime after the Wynn Family moved to 1408 North Alabama Street, an event occurred , Which, although belonging more properly to the article to follow this than here, is worthy of notice because of its importance in relation to Topsey. One afternoon Dr. Wynn came home to dinner with an enigmatical expression on his face which had the various members of the family (Topsey included) thoroughly mystified. Even when he presented a cigar box to the young harum-scarum, the mystery was as profound as ever to all except Topsey, who was all excitement and. whined knowingly. The suspense was broken when the young harum-scarum thoughtlessly turned the box upside down. Immediately an uncanny scratching came from the box, and a moment later a high, whimpering mew. The truth of tie matter at last found its way through the thick skull of the harum-scarum and he carried the precious box up stairs where he opened it on a bed.. A scared, ruffled little something, more resembling a last year's muff than a kitten, came rolling out all in a heap. For a moment it blinked its eyes stupidly at the light. Then, starting in its throat that miniature saw—mill, peculiar to very little kittens, it to toddled across the bed to meet the young harum-scarum. But Topsey, feeling herself called upon to defend herself and her title as household favorite, rushed valiantly toward the enemy. Who knows but that she deemed herself the Champion of suffrage and so felt inspired to employ her utmost courage in defending the glory of the cause from the invasion of a mere man—kitten? But alas, the attack failed. The newcomer, by some distinctly cattish writhe drew his little back into a graceful bow, and followed this remarkable feat by emitting a series of convulsive hisses from his tiny throat,--a performance which was equally amazing and bewildering to the astonished Topsey. It was too much: With dropped head and tail, she beat a hasty retreat down the stairway. But she was not permanently beaten. She soon reapproached the stranger, but this time with a conciliatory attitude. This policy proved so successful that she and the kitten were soon on the best of terms. So warn did the friendship grow that Topsey became almost a foster mother to the little orphan. (One cold winter morning she actually assumed the responsibility of carrying Tommy, the kitten, into the house from the front porch where lie had, been enjoying an early morning promenade.

Several years the animals were the principals in a como—tragedy which was at once one of the most aggravating but humorous of occurrences. It happened t the Wynn home at 1406 North Alabama Street. In passing, it may he well to say that the house into which the Wynnses moved at 1408 was quite a remarkable old edifice because of the interesting variety of respects in which it was thoroughly run down. The wall paper in several of the rooms would have disgraced an Indiana Avenue saloon, while the woodwork seemed afflicted with a horrible disease which caused its varnish to peel off in ugly blisters with extremely disastrous effects to the interior beauty of the structure. The stairway, a victim of' the same malady, was so far gone that it might have passed for a remnant of pioneer days, so frightfully discolored were its steps. In the face of this discouraging prospect, Dr. Wynn nobly volunteered to renovate the stairway with a coat of varnish. It was on that eventful day that our present incident occurred. The worthy doctor was almost through; he was, in fact, putting the finishing touches on the last step, when the screen door slammed and that patrician bit of dog flesh, Topsey, went innocently pitty-pattying up the sticky stairway before the horrified painter could offer resistance. With an exclamation of astonishment and rage, the doctor brandished his dripping paint brush menacingly. Topsey, who had gone half way up stairs, eyed him quizzicaliy. Knowing nothing else to do, the wrathful- doctor bawled. out in deep, stentorian bass the one word, Topsey!! The stern appellation resounded through the hail with awful solemnity, and Topsey, going up two steps farther, sat down with a sickening squash. This was indeed a trying situation, a disagreeable culmination for both dog and man! Fortunately, the peace angel here put in an appearance in the person of Mrs. Wynn. This individual was so thoroughly convulsed with laughter that she quite forgot the seriousness of the situation. A gentle word from her brought the scared puppy down stairs immediately, where that matchless compound,—soap and water, and elbow grease, made short work of Topsey' s disfiguration which fortunately was not great since the varnish had for the most part dried. The one exclamation "Meooow!" from the head of the stairs immediately turned all eyes to the spot where the veteran Tom stood, evidently trying to make up his mind whether or' not to descend. Of course he came down, and a new chain of foot prints adorned tile already highly decorated stairway. As has been said before, tile varnish was so nearly dry that little permanent damage was done to the stage of this, little drama of daily life. The actors, too, were none the worse for wear, save Topsey, who was somewhat disconcerted by her bath of soapsuds and water, and Torn, who spent the rest of the afternoon alternately sneezing and licking his highly scented feet. This incident has since been accorded a position of preeminence in the Wynnses' Hall of Reminiscences whence it has been often recalled to grace many a conversation when animals were tile subject of consideration.

As the years have elapsed, Topsey has undergone several marked. changes. She has lost her graceful symmetry of form, and, although her face is still as attractive as ever, her body bears a close resemblance to an exaggerated stovepine. She is the counterpart of the dogs in a toy Noah's Ark with regard to tail, for that part of her anatomy looks quite as if it had been thrust in by a careless toymaker, utterly devoid of the artistic sense. The Wynnses do not hesitate to attribute Topsey's bodily grossness to their own carelessness in spoiling her. Probably all of her changes are due to this same source.

The advent of the automobile into the Wynnses' daily life marked the beginning of a new epoch in the history of Topsey's life. On the eventful day on which the transaction occurred, she conceived it to be her duty to act as guardian of the machine. She has acted upon her conviction ever since. She rides everywhere and anywhere she can get a chance to go regardless of whether or not she has received any special invitation. In fact, she has become so thoroughly wedded to the machine that she enjoys merely sitting in it while it is stationary almost as much as riding. Consequently, it is the usual sight to see her adorning the mechanician's seat at most any time of the day or night that the machine is in front of the house.

The young harum-scarum has been heard to say that he thought Topsey enjoyed the Wynn machine quite as much as she did the Wynn family. There may be some truth In this, for one afternoon when the machine was not in its accustomed place in front of the house, she signified her disregard for the Wynn family by independently climbing into a neighbor's automobile. The neighbor, who had witnessed the whole performance, started toward his machine with an illegible expression on his face, which doubtless portended no good for Topsey. But she,with intuitive canine judgment, absconded before the storm broke. After all the Wynnses were bettor off for Topsey's adventure, for since, she has been less heady in her choice of machines. Still the auto continues to hold a position of all—importance in Topsey's sphere of activities.

It was in an automobile experience that Topsey first signified her general dislike for gentlemen of color. On one of Dr. Wynn's lecture evenings at the medical college Topsey had been permitted to ride down with him. When the machine had nearly reached the college something went wrong with the gear shift, and the doctor was compelled to leave the machine at the nearest garage (which happened to he operated by dusky mechanics). Topsey took in the situation with interest; she watched from her perch in the back seat. The doctor gave instructions for the car to be driven over to the medical college when fixed, and then left. After the usual amount of sweating and pounding, the two dusky workmen took their seats in front and started for the medical college. Topsey could hardly believe her eyes. Were these plebeian wretches expecting her, the distinguished queen of her race, to ride with them? What could they be doing with her machine anyhow? The affair looked so ominous that Topsey, without a second thought, leaped out. Under ordinary circumstances, a fall from a speeding auto to the street would have humiliated her, but this was no ordinary matter, and off she sped at full speed. The horrified gentlemen of color gave chase in the machine; but what is a mere auto when the distinguished Topsey is inclined o run? The dusky mechanics gave up the chase and prepared to make the best of the matter before the doctor. As a result of the affair that individual was bluer as he rode home that night than he had been in many a day; for he pictured to himself innumerable calamities which might befall the lost dog during her meanderings on the down town streets. But his fears were short lived. Upon returning home, he found Topsey waiting for him quite as she had waited for him long ago after her elopement with the postman.

She had merely come home, disgusted that her master should allow strangers to drive her about.

There are only two features in Topsey's routine of life which are really unpleasant. One when the Wynnses go away on a trip; the other, when she has to be clipped. On the former occasion, she wanders aimlessly about the neighborhood, usually haunting the spots where children are at play. During the Wynnses' traveling season, she is an object of universal pity throughout the locality.

Getting clipped is even a more strenuous experience for her. She trembles so violently and pants so spasmodically that it is a matter requiring considerable skill to cut all hair and no dog. Then, too, her figure is so distorted with fat that rolling over is for her a decidedly difficult feat. Everything considered, it does not seen strange that Topsey should believe her term of mortal existence at an end when she is hoisted onto the clipping table; that is unquestionably her feeling, for even though some member of the family stays near to pacify her, she vociferates a few measures of canticle which might well pass for a cannibal funeral dirge.

Topsey's reputation as a watchdog is grossly overestimated. In this respect all the evidence is against her. The one and only burglar that the Wynnses ever had got in without the slightest suspicion of such a thing entering Topsey's mind. He would probably have stolen the very roof off the house without Topsey's so much as dreaming of such a thing, had not Dr. Wynn unwittingly frightened him off by going upstairs to prepare for a banquet. She has been known to kill a rat once, and there are some theories extant that she has made other ventures in this dangerous field of activity; but unfortunately, convincing proofs are lacking. Topsey is also very much afraid of anything of an explosive nature; consequently, a thunder storm puts her into untold agonies. Indeed, if there is but the most infinitesimal fraction of a black cloud in the sky, Topscy teases to come into the house. (In this respect, she is quite an accurate barometer). It must be admitted that, despite her assumed bravery, Topsey is considerable of a bluffer.

But let us pass lightly over the shortcomings of Topsey; for there is so much commendable about her that she merits our respect. And now, as the young harum-scarum concludes the penning of this biography (for it is no other than he who has been describing Topsey), it is with a feeling of pride and satisfaction in being possessed of such a companion that he proposes this closing health to Topsey:

"May her days be many and merry ere the arrival of that final, one on which he must take pen to append to this article its epilogue, Topsey's epitaph.

THE CAREER OF MR. THOMAS WYNN

Mr. Thomas, before his arrival at the Wynnses', resided on the south side with his mother and numerous brothers and sisters. Hi mother was a fine pussy cat of the Maltese species, and her children were excellent of feline aristocracy. The whole Family's prosperity was probably due, in a large measure, to the kindness of a little boy at whose home the cat family made its domicile. But it was decreed by fate that the little company was not to remain united. The first step toward the breaking of family ties was the result of an illness of the little boy when he became so sick that a doctor's attention seemed necessary, he was put to bed, and the cat family was distributed about the counterpane to keep him company. Thus, the attending physician struck up quite a warm acquaintance with the little invalid's playfellows, who were constantly mixing up in childish combats and clawless sparring matches in the folds of the bed—clothes. When the little boy finally recovered, the doctor bill was paid in kitten instead of money. The little boy's family was not in the best of circumstances financially, so Tommy came to be a member of the Wynn family, for the attending physician was no other than Dr. Wynn.

It will be remembered from the previous article, that shortly after Tommy's arrival at the Wynnses', there was a council of war held between him and Topsey. It will also be remembered that the result of this conference was somewhat humiliating to Topsey; but she soon forgot her shameful reception of Tommy on the first day, for he was inclined to be friendly in spite of her coldness. In fact, before long, Topsey forgot her own dignity to such an extent that she allowed herself to race around after, and maul the kitten quite as good-naturedly as his brothers had played with him a few weeks before. The Wynnses soon found themselves in possession of a menagerie—vaudeville which held daily performances in the sitting room and parlor, and occasionally on the front porch. These porch entertainments became a source of great amusement to the neighbors.

But Tommy did not depend on Topsey to act as his supernumerary in all of his stunts. He actually had the audacity to employ Dr. Wynn in this capacity for one caper, "cut" when the family would eat dinner. Whenever at dinner or supper time Tom felt especially hungry or sociable, it was his custom to leap dexterously on Dr. Wynn's shoulder and there spend the remainder of the meal time. If very hungry, he would tuck his head along the side of the doctor's collar and purr most affectionately; but if he had mounted his perch for social sake alone, he would crouch down across the narrow ledge of the doctor's shoulders and assume the air of a mighty monarch reviewing his subjects from a lofty throne of gold. It was this attitude that won for him the name King Tom of Catland, a sobriquet which was given him by Ellsworth Olcott, a chum of the young harum-scarum , and a great lover of cats. As Tommy approached young manhood his nerve increased to a surprising degree until he actually embellished the old trick of jumping on the doctor's with a startling addiction, a leap from Dr. Wynn's shoulder to that of the young harum-scarum who sat at an adjacent side of the rectangular table. Although this feat was quite unusual and awe-inspiring, it was prohibited at the earnest solicitation of Mrs. Wynn; for Tom's aerial course during the process of this leap, lay directly over that particular corner of the table where the potato dish held forth. Thus the first check was placed upon the activities of Thomas and Wynnses Acrobatic Troupe.

Perhaps it would have been better then and there to eliminate all dining- room capers; for even the plain shoulder jumping wrought havoc one night at a dinner party to which several of Dr. Wynn's professional friends and their wives were invited. Dr. and Mrs. heath were among the guests , and. Mrs. Wynn had by happens, seated Mrs. Heath at the place usually occupied by the doctor of our household. When the meal had progressed as far as the salad course, the company was startled by the sound of a plaintive mew from someplace under the table. Mrs. Wynn turned white: Tommy had evidently escaped from his place of temporary confinement. But she had no time to act. A moment after announcing his arrival, he made his company debut in an even more spectacular manner by suddenly appearing on Mrs. Heath's shoulder. She was startled to say the least, but no more so than Tommy who had leaped before he looked, expecting to land on the doctor of his own acquaintance. As it was, he stared helplessly at the strangers with big, scared eyes of mute appeal, and then awkwardly returned to the floor. Ever since, he has been more or less chary of his visits to Dr. Wynn's shoulder. The commotion of that one evening made quite an impression upon Tom.

As Torn entered the age of young manhood, he became in many senses of the word a "fast liver." He came to be a regular actor in the feline grand opera productions rendered nightly at the Ogden Street Grand Opera House. (Ogden Street Is the alley between New Jersey and Alabama Streets.) At about this time he entered-the order of active feline pugilists, for he returned one morning from an expedition with his insignia of membership, a slit ear. Mrs. Wynn hereupon conceived the notion that a bath might be of benefit to the young reprobate, both in checking the increase in the population of live stock upon his person and in curbing his rash, aggressive spirit. The experiment worked beautifully in achieving the first result, but it was not so successful with the second. The youthful highflier was frightened into meekness during his sojourn in the tub, but once back on the floor, he signified his triumph by spitting and growling so ferociously that the young harum-scarum, who was down on the front porch, heard plainly the strenuous dialogue between Tommy and his mistress. Surely it is a degenerate young man who will so impolitely dispute his foster mother when she is voluntarily giving him a much-needed bath.

In those days, Tornmy's "character" was only in the formative state. Now he has settled down to be a gentleman of strong Convictions. One of these is his right in choice of front porch chairs.

No matter how kittenish and affectionate he may be as he rolls over and cuts up generally in his romps with different members of the family in the back yard, (He is especially partial to Mrs. Wynn) he will plainly assert his rights if any member of the family happens to take the chair he wants on the front porch. This he does by either sitting on the floor in front of the offender and plainly scowling his dissatisfaction, or else by even standing on his hind legs by the side of the coveted chair as if in contemplation of making it his in spite of its occupant. It disgusts him more than ever to be escorted from a chair he already occupies, and consequently, Dr. Wynn regularly acts as such an escorter every morning. ("Perversity, thy name is 'Wynn"") Tom has never yet been known to release his claim to the chair peaceably. It is only after he has publicly announced his abuses to the world in general that he withdraws.

If any strange animal comes onto the Wynnses porch and Tom is aware of the fact, there is sure to be an interesting situation develop, for Tom will not for a moment tolerate the intrusion. A year or so ago, a neighbor made the Wynnses a porch call. She came accompanied by her brother's pet bull dog. The dog remained on the steps most of the time, only coming on the porch at the close of the visit. Tom, aroused by the pattering of feet, took in the situation instantly and at once descended from the chair where he had been napping. After allowing his tail to swell to proper dimensions, he rose upon his hind feet and sallied into the bull dog bear fashion. The dog was clearly dumbfounded. He had considered his visage alone a sure guard against molestation from even pugilists of' his own race. (From my point of view, he seemed thoroughly justified in entertaining this belief.) Tom's teeth and claws were soon working with such efficiency on the dog's tender nose that the latter turned tail and fled home. At this juncture, Topsey's summoned courage enough to charge from her refuge behind Mrs. Wynn's chair to the edge of the porch where she barked valiantly at the retreating form of the enemy. But Tom did not care to have his own glory lessened by such a notorious bluff as Topsey, so he gave her also a box on the nose, which sent her whining under the settee. After this final act of bravery, he stalked back to his chair to receive with great dignity and condescension the compliments of his family. Thus it may plainly be seen that Tom is a creature self-reliant, depending neither upon Topsey nor the family for his maintenance and protection. It is the pride of his family, especially the young harum-scarum, that he is such; and although they love the simple duties of taking care of him, they are much gratified to know that he is still capable of managing himself. Indeed, the old veteran is quite as lively as he was in his youth, and not nearly so frivolous as then.

MOUNT RAINIER, WASHINGTON

(Editors note: This is an account of climbing with the Mazamas Mountaineering Club in Washington's Mount Rainier Park. No date was recorded in the title section of this entry in James Wynn's original journal. In Chapter III below, James compares a section of this climb to one in the Canadian Rockies in 1914, suggesting that this trip occurred at least a year or so later. However, the comical narrative composed as Chapter VI of this trip in Rainier Park is "copyrighted" in 1914. Because Chapter VI is obviously a fictitious story with references to Frederick Cooks claims of reaching the North Pole that many at the time thought was fabricated, James may have actually written the account after 1914, but set the copyright date back to add to the fabrication effect of the concocted story.)

Chapter I

From Tacoma to Moraine Park

Yes, no doubt about its being Sunday morning Church bells throughout Tacoma announced the fact with discordant jangle. But when Father and I finally clattered down the stairs of the Tacoma Hotel to the main lobby, we lacked our white collars, stiff shirts, highly'-polished shoes, and the rest of our usual church—going paraphernalia. No, dear reader, though you be the president of a foreign missionary society, I cannot but make my confession: we were not going to church. Our costumes alone would have created too great a furor in the fashion circles of any congregation. Duxback coats and trousers, canvas leggings and hobnailed shoes would hardly pass the Ladies' Home Journal standards as "in vogue" for the church pew. No, we were about to enter Mazamadon We were about to get back to our old mountain ways after a long year's absence in office and laboratory

Father, greatly elated at the tact, was positively frisky. He started gleefully toward the dining room with the air of a kitten, just released to frolic in the back-yard after a night in a stuffy back porch. That reckless start was entirely unworthy a practiced mountaineer. A slick floor immediately made of it an impromptu hobnail "glissade" which would have done credit to any vaudeville acrobat. After Father had finally righted himself and the suppressed giggles of the Japanese bell boys had subsided, we entered the dining room with greater caution and more becoming dignity, quite convinced that a tile floor is no fitting stage for kitten gambols.

The breakfast hour passed quickly, for we met our old Hoosier friend, Pres. Stone of Purdue University, and spent the tine gossiping with him quite as it we had not met for years. After hastily swallowing our allotment of diminutive pancakes, we rounded up our dunnage rolls and climbing implements at the Union Station. Then came the train ride to Fairfax with a seeming host of Mazamas, bedecked with various insignia and ribbons, clad in outfits not unlike our own.

To us, the ride was naturally a somewhat bewildering one, for we knew scarcely anyone of the merry crowd which surged through the car. About the only two faces which stand out clearly in my memory of that ride are those of Miss Henthorne, formerly of our Indianapolis Library, and Dr. Barck, a curious little German front St. Louis. He talked very interestingly of his climbing experience (which was quite ample) but I am ashamed to confess I was not so engrossed by what he said as how he said it. Never have I heard a voice which so quaintly united the bravado of the German with the deliberate of the Switzer. Besides his queer manner of speaking , the Doctor had a way of half shrugging his shoulders, tilting his head, and savagely scratching his bearded cheek. Curious mannerisms they were and so distinctly Barekian as to be quite inimitable.

Two hours later, when we had finally rumbled into Fairfax and Dr. Barck, after having wished us a "bleasant drip", had slouched down the aisle, we clambered out, bristling with alpenstock and ice ax. Before boarding the logging train which was to bear us to its terminus, a point farther up on the Carbon River, we had a short glance at Fairfax. The place is by no means prepossessing in appearance, but it is worthy of mention, for it is a fair prototype of the many lumber towns of the North—west. A large mill, a number of dingy, unpainted houses, a "general store" --these plus a few saloons and plenty of forest fire smoke and you have Fairfax, a typical working center for the development of our western lumber districts.

Prom Fairfax we enjoyed a five mile joggle up a logging railroad on a train of flat cars, on which the entire Mazama following—some one hundred and twenty in all—collected. The ride was hardly eventful in the strict sense of the word, though the air was kept constantly ringing with the Mazama yell and outbursts of "near-melody". Our little caricature of a logging engine contributed its part to the entertainment by panting most asthmatically all the way up; finally it went even so far as to jump the track in its effort to keep up the excitement.

Once at the end of the logging road, we tumbled off the flat car as gracefully as circumstances would permit, and proceeded at once to a point on the banks of the Carbon River only a few hundred yards distant. This was the noon lunch stop. Here, after some complicated maneuvering, I managed to capture a bun, a peach, and a pickle. These I carefully "Fletcherized" until they seemed like heavy repast.

Shortly after scoring a triumph over my pickle I slung on the rucksack, seized my alpenstock, and started up the gradual trail alone, since Father remained behind with Dr. Stone. The first two hours of the hike through the forest dragged heavily, not only because of the meagerness of my breakfast and lunch, but also because of the previous week of idleness which I had spent in train riding. However, about three in the afternoon Second Wind came to the rescue and I began to swing into my old stride and to enjoy the wonderful trees among which our trail lay.

The charm of one of these virgin mountain forests is truly supernatural in its subtleness. Trees, trees, everywhere trees. There are giant cedars, some tall, severely upright, and others leaning uncertain against their neighbors, groaning at even the mildest zephyr. Then there are the spruce, perhaps a trifle less imposing, with their gummy sides and sticky wealth of greenery; trees of all sizes and shapes, standing, leaning, arching, and reclining. some are sound, others rotten; some clean-'barked, others garbed with a shroud of moldy moss and bristling with fungi. Of course, each tree tells its story, presents its attractions ,and makes its appeal yet the charm of the forest lies deeper. It is not in any one of these, yet it pervades all,—that subtle Something, perceptible but incomprehensible, to be sensed but not analyzed. Ours is but to feel it, glory in it, and thank God for it.

Through just such a forest with just such an inexplicable fascination about it, I trudged until shortly after five o'clock, only coming to the open now and then along the rock strewn bed of the Carbon River.

Then, having gradually worked my way over the excellent trail well up toward the head— waters of the Carbon, I came suddenly into an arched enclosure, in the very heart of a giant group of trees. Two cabins, a small group of weary Mazamas, a crackling fire, and a jolly, red—faced cook plainly bespoke the place as Independence Camp.

Father arrived somewhat later, and we spent the rest of the evening munching camp lunch, adjusting our luggage, and opening the sleeping role. One brief moment that we enjoyed shortly after supper repaid us a hundred—fold for the labor of the day. From a point in the Carbon River bed not a great distance from camp we saw, a short distance to the north—east, vague and mysterious in the twilight, "Old He" himself - Tahoma, filmed by that same ghost mantle which at evening enshrouds the greater peaks of both American Rockies and Cascades. For only a moment we gazed on the vision—like reality; then "To bed "from Father, and we began a night of genuine sleep, undisturbed by street car bells or auto horns.

At about quarter after four the next morning some considerate mosquito gently aroused me by a morning serenade. Though it was still dark I hastily slid out of the sleeping bag, unconsciously bringing Father with me. For several moments we sat blinking at the "cavern" revealed by the flickering fire of "Doc" Weston the camp cook. Here, in truth was an ideal setting for the "Peer Gynt" scene in the main hail of the Troll King's mountain palace, The shadowed ground might well have passed for the marble floor of the palace; the ghostly trees for the shadowed alabaster pillars; the black above for the vaulted arches; Doc Weston's fire for the flaming alter of the mountain deity. Truly marvelous in its setting was this natural theatre. Could only the blood—chilling measures of Grieg's matchless D minor— the Troll Dance have echoed through these natural corridors and this outdoor stage would have been worthy the histrionic skill of Louis James himself—the master interpreter of Ibsen.

I came down from the clouds with a thump when the odor of Doc Weston's pancakes was suddenly wafted over our sleeping bag. Even Ibsen and Grieg must gracefully retire when the king of the commissary thus issues his call. It was but the work of a few minutes to bind up our sleeping bag, leave it near the pack train, and "stock up" on pork-potato—pancake breakfast. Then once more to the trail, the dear old trail, where I can forget, test—tubes, Bunsen burners, spectroscopes, and all the rest of it, and get back to the Open!

The first part of the morning we spent in ascending the vast treminal and lower medial moraines of the Carbon Glacier, the great ice river which, unlike the majority of the glaciers of Tahoma, has its head in a glacial cirque at the base of Willis Wall, the precipice front of the

Mountain on the north side. The climbing of this morainal deposit was comparatively easy, for the advance party of the Mazama scouts had marked the trail unmistakably.

Aside from the Mountain itself, of which we caught only momentary glances because of gathering mists, the most notable features of the ascent were the beautiful ice cave at the snout of' the Carbon Glacier, and the milky water which issued from this cave aperture. The milky tinge to the water is due ,of course, to the presence of the suspended silica which the glacier is constantly and mercilessly grinding off the rocks in its path. As I examined the matter which settled from a cup of this water I could not help wondering at the ease with which Nature performs feats which are the chemist's bug bear. There, at the bottom of the cup was almost pure silicon dioxide, ground finer than I had been able to pulverize a specimen in the laboratory a few months before with the best of iron mortars:

When well up on the glacier's lower reaches we veered to the south—east into the parkland where in the rapidly gathering mist and drizzling rain, we completely lost view of the mountain and many of the nearer ridges. However, we pushed hastily on, refreshed by the mists and cooling rain, yet kept dry by our bulky duxback coats.

Parklands or natural garden spots occur on almost all sides of Tahoma, just below and between the projecting snouts of the glaciers, but of all the parklands we saw on the north or south of Tahoma, none, except possibly Sotolick's Hunting Ground, could compare in vernal charm and pastoral grace with moraine Park. Before surmounting the two final ridges separating the Carbon Glacier from Moraine Park, we passed through numerous parklets verdant with mosses and grasses of the most exquisite shades of green and blue. In the midst of heterogeneous banks of flowers, countless mountain lilies (Xerophyllum Tenax) with their fluffy, yellow—white heads, dotted the rich green of these undulating parklets, and here and there a whole knoll would be tinted a brilliant red by gorgeous banks of Indian Paintbrush (Castillira oreopala). Even in the rapidly settling mountain mists the gorgeousness of the floral color scheme seemed scarcely dimmed.

Through just such flower—studded areas we proceeded until within twenty minutes of Camp Prouty. This last stretch lay over two ridges. Once having traversed these, we dropped rapidly down a grassy slope to the shores of Mystic Lake, where Camp Prouty, the Mazama Camp, was located. Rapidly moving clouds of fine rain made it impossible for us to form any first impression of the scenic phases of the camp site. We were content, however, to visit the commissary tent before feasting on any more scenery. After a light lunch (which was, in truth, a luxurious one compared to the average camper's fare) we retired to the tent which Mr. Prouty, the hospitable Mazama president, insisted on our taking. Though dripping and somewhat soggy, we were in a far from dull-weather frame of mind. A gentle rain to settle the forest tire smoke; a picturesque lake to camp by; a matchless commissary department to rely on; true Mazama nature lovers to hike with! Even the worst pessimist would have broken his own wretched faith under such circumstances.

Chapter II

An afternoon scramble on Moraine Bluffs.

Once bitten by the "mountain bug", Father can hardly keep still long enough to eat and sleep. Consequently, we had hardly been in the tent half an hour when he sagely remarked that we might as well hike in our wet duxback as sit still. The rain had stopped and the low—lying clouds, lifting with amazing rapidity, revealed a rugged little cliff with an almost sheer face of eight hundred or a thousand feet, towering over the valley on the south side. Fate surely seemed to have had a hand in revealing that cliff just when she did: it presented just what e wanted — easy "limber-up" material for an afternoon hike.

Before starting up the bluff we wandered through the camp where we were joined by two Mazamas who were destined to become the warmest of our friends and the most constant of our hiking companions ---Mr. Howard and Miss Anne Dillinger, both of Portland. Both impressed us at once as being ideal mountaineering chums. Mr. Howard had the long, wiry build of one fit, in every sense of the word, for the most strenuous of climbs. Then, too, he had an irresistible frankness about him and a way of laughing off all petty grievances which plainly marked him as a man among men. When I first met Anne —or, as I called her, "Miss Dillinger" —I was in a measure astounded. Could it be possible? Was this another Dora Keene? Yes, woolen socks, climbing boots, and a scarred alpenstock all plainly told their story. Here, to all appearances, was a woman climber of the first order!

But still I was skeptical. In nine years of climbing I had never known one of the other sex to "make good" on the rocks. Had not even the hearty New York suffragette—athlete gone to pieces on the upper crags of Mt. Fairview, a very easy climb in the Canadian Rockies at Laggan? She whom I had thought a fair climber had not even lasted to ten thousand feet on a mountain where "chimney relaying" is unknown

All the time I was carrying on this mental debate we had been gradually working our way around to the back of the bluff which I call

Moraine Crags. (It has not yet been officially named.) Just before starting up the final rock slope we beheld an interesting figure coming over a hillock behind us. She might have passed for one of the fat German women that visit our Indianapolis market, except for the fact that she carried an alpenstock instead of a basket.

Noticing us pause ,she shouted to go ahead. She would catch up, she said. And what a voice "hers" was Me Hercule! Surely no woman could ever have been the possessor of such vocal cords. Then a gust of wind cleared the seeming inconsistency by blowing aside the skirt like sweater which dangled about her feet, and the veil—like mosquito netting covering her head. The lady was Mr. Robinson of Portland, a good—natured novice at climbing, who had been trailing us from camp. Anne promptly dubbed him "Lady Robinson of the Green Veil" and for the rest of the short climb he acted as official caboose to our party.

After sighting him we climbed for shortly over ten minutes and then found ourselves on the insignificant summit of the cliff. Where we spent several minutes viewing Mystic Lake from different crags of the cliff crest. Presently Lady Robinson joined us, puffing like the poor logging engine that had served us so nobly after leaving Fairfax. After mopping her tomato-hued visage Lady Robinson proceeded to gaze on the lake beneath us as best she could from her point of observation some six feet from the edge of the cliff.

The presence of fine mist clouds in the atmosphere made photography out of the question; so we began cautiously to work our way down the front of the cliff by means of a rock chute --somewhat on the order of the basaltic chimneys so common in Canada; this, however, was not so precipitous. Though fairly steep and somewhat tiring in places because of the necessity of testing the rock, the route we followed was readily negotiable, and we made good time lead by the Professor. (Thus Anne had christened Father, little guessing the truth of her assertion, though I hardly think the dignified senior medics of a few months before would have liked to acknowledge their Professor of Physical Diagnosis in his present far from scholastic garb.)

When almost down the cliff, just after rounding a somewhat treacherous crag, I gazed back for a moment at Lady Robinson. Queer as it seemed to me at the time the fact remained undeniable that the real lady of our party was fast distancing the lady of the Green Veil. Yes, Anne negotiated the descent with such ease and perfect self—command that I then and there ousted from my mind the conviction that had been forming for almost nine years. Here at least was one feminine worthy to wear the jaunty feather so prized by Rudolph Aemmer, my Swiss chum on Mt. Temple. Here, at least, was one worthy a place in the rope line of

Fritz Browand, the rock expert at Field, B.C. Once back to my tent I set down in my notes a platitude which a year before I would have laughed to scorn:

"SOME WOMEN CAN CLIMB."

Yes, Silvia Highheel, you living fashion plate of the summer hotel veranda or the sea—side dance hail, there are at least some of your sex who have learned what unsurpassed joys are to be found in the great out—of—doors, —- some who, bucking up against the Wild in all its ruggedness have come to realize the truth of my friend Eddie Sammons' statement, "This is the life"

Chapter III

A Day on the Carbon Glacier.

The day following our Moraine Bluff hike was dazzling in its brilliancy a brilliancy peculiar to altitudes far removed from city smoke or sea level mists. For the first time we beheld the north face of the mountain under really favorable circumstances. The stupendous amphitheater of the Carbon glacial cirque stood out with that distinctness only possible in atmosphere comparatively tree from water vapor. White as the foam of an ocean wave were the vast snow neves heaped up on the crest of Willis Wall. Even in the best season such days as this are rare. Hence the Professor, Anne, and I lost no time in starting for the Carbon Glacier which we had previously determined to explore.

It was on this day's tramp that we met two more climbers who were destined to become our fellow Mazarnettes. Our course lay over a low ridge adjoining Moraine Bluffs, and it was on this ridge that we first met Messrs. Barnes and Philips. For Barnes the Professor and I could not but feel a particular bond of friendship: he was a native Hoosier, in fact, an Indianapolis Hoosier ---the brother of Dr. Barnes, one of the Professor's former students. To the frequenters of Rainier Park this Mr. Barnes (C. A. Barnes, of Tacoma) needs no more introduction than A. H. Barnes, the other photographer, for both have seen old Tahoma in almost every mood and from almost every side. At this particular time Barnes and his companion Philips were camping in a rangers cabin a short distance above Camp Prouty. On this day, having no particular plan, they readily joined us, and our little group of five continued up the Moraine Bluff ridge with the plan in view of following its crest to the south—west, where it converges with the great lateral moraine extending north—west from the Mountain and bounding the east side of the Carbon Glacier.

When we finally gained the crest of this lateral moraine we held the key to the topography of the Carbon Glacier, Willis Wall, and the several cleaver ribs protruding from the north face of the wall. Time has worked a peculiar change in the structure of this eastern moraine. At first glance one might think it extended up the mountain itself, forming an integral part of the lava spine charted as the Carbon—Winthrop-cleaver. However, even a cursory examination of the character of the rock will plainly indicate that this moraine—cleaver ridge is not homogeneous. At lower altitudes it is composed of countless rocks of all sizes, but all are very hard and bear the unmistakable smoothness of surface which marks them as part of the glaciers dump heap. Farther up on the ridge the rock is entirely different in character. Though quite slaggy in appearance – in fact, almost scoriae—like —these upper lava ridges undoubtedly contain a high per cent of silica. At no place on the lava stretches of the Carbon—Winthrop Cleaver did I discover any really large crystalline deposits. This is hardly to be expected, however, in lavas of distinctly acid reaction and not of the porphyritic structure.

When Barnes and the Professor had satisfied themselves Photographically concerning the panorama laid out before us, we concocted some miserable jargon which we formally established under a pile of rock. After this all important part of the climb, We descended the ridge on the glacier side, gradually working toward the mountain and ever keeping lookout for negotiable "leads" on to the glacier. Finally at the base of the moraine, we were about to venture out on the glacier by a route which promised to be at once negotiable and "interesting", when a faint shout reached us from the ridge crest, and on to it two tiny figures bobbed into sharp relief against the dark blue sky. By the time we had succeeded in making small hand nooses in our rope, the two new—corners had successfully descended and were ready to join us in the rope line. They were our friend Howard of the Moraine Bluffs hike and Mr. Hitch, an attorney of Portland.

In working our way toward the central ice fields of the glacier, we encountered almost every variety of ice wall and crevasse. For the first hour or more our progress was rapid. Although we were constantly ascending and descending crevasse ridges and occasionally back—tracking to avoid impassable chasms the entire surface of the ice was covered by a layer of morainal gravel which made step cutting seldom necessary - and step cutting is usually the bug-bear of glacier exploration.

As we traversed one ridge after another and there still seemed to be no sign of our reaching areas of greater inclination, I could not help contrasting the present climb - or, rather, "ice walk" with our 1914 ascent of the Illecilewaet, the so-called big glacier of Canada. Though it is not nearly so large as the Carbon, it is so steep, its sides so free from morainal debris that reaching its crest in some places is considered quite a feat. Occasionally the ice wall is so precipitate that climbers are all but forced to the expedient of cutting holes for the hands as well as the feet.

Little over an hour of travel over this dirt be1t of the Carbon brought us well into the ice stream's interior, where we began some mild but genuine ice climbing. For the rest of the morning the climbing was almost all of this sort - over glare ice fields, comparatively level but extremely "cut up" by parallel crevasses.

By noon we reached the more remote regions of the glacier, higher up and farther back toward Willis Wall. Here we felt justified in dispensing with our rope, for the glacial surface began to assume the appearance of vast neves through which a relatively small number of crevasses were open, though grayish depressions in the snow surface plainly indicated the presence of hidden chasms. It is to these apparently harmless snow fields that Willis Wall really owes its existence. Doubtless they originally covered a less abrupt rock slope, the original of Willis Wall. Snow falls are much heavier at moderately high altitudes than on the mountain's summit. Hence these head neves of the Carbon were constantly replenished by fresh snows. The drifts formed by these were subjected to the constant routine of thawing and freezing during the sun's heat and the night's frigidity. when we consider the tremendous physical force of this action, the pressure which this constant contraction and expansion would have on the supporting rock races beneath the neves, we can readily see how the Carbon Glacier has thus literally gnawed out, as Mr. Matthes says, the great cirque—like amphitheater forming the western hollow of Willis Wall. The very snow neves over which we crunched. were the makers of the colossal precipice overhanging them.

But unfortunately we could not push on much farther. The Professor, having forgotten his amber goggles, wisely stopped on a projecting pile of rock, fearing that his eyes might again become as painfully snow—bitten as they had been on Mt. Temple the year before. The rest of us hastened on quite a distance, but it is not good policy to scatter out in groups of less than three when on a glacier. Hence Anne and I, leaving the other four to penetrate the still more remote fastnesses of the neves, returned to where we had left the Professor.

The direct rays of the sun were off the lower reaches of the glacier; so toward these extremely jagged stretches of ice we directed our steps. For nearly two hours we penetrated as crazy a conglomeration of ice pinnacles and chasms as I have ever seen. The crevasses in this section of the Carbon, though not as colossal as some of the higher fissure of the Winthrop, are certainly as numerous and as extensively corniced. The

Professor was so dazed that he performed his characteristic stunt of losing his spectacles; consequently he had the privilege of retracing his steps for almost half a mile to where he had left them, carefully folded up on a little ledge of rock.

The Professor photographed this arctic wonderland quite extensively, but because of the glaring contrast of light and shadow, the results proved to be very disappointing. As we have found in most of our excursions to mountain land, the true glory and wonder of it all can live in memory alone.

When finally we left the glacier, it was at a point far below the reach over which we had entered. During our five hours of exploration we had described a great circle, the circumference of which traversed almost every variety of ice or snow surface the glacier had to offer. We had seen the Carbon in almost all of its phases.

Once having left the glacier we scaled the moraine wall which overlooks Mystic Lake from the west. Here we paused only a few minutes just long enough to plan our course down the steep side of the moraine. Though the Professor with his characteristic aversion to snow preferred to keep to the rock, Anne and I ventured out on a vast snow field which slanted down at a very considerable angle, suddenly disappearing behind a slight hillock in the snow some distance ahead. Anne crouching skillfully on her alpenstock glissaded rapidly down and over the snow hillock, completely out of sight with only a fine cloud of glistening snow particles to mark where she had vanished. I skated down the incline as best I could "stand—up—fashion". True glissading was out of the question, for my alpenstock had no hide string in the end, and I dared not risk the one suit of clothes I had in any rash adventure. Below the hillock the snow slope had an even greater inclination than before; so the last quarter of a mile was genuine sport. Despite the No. 8 ice calks in my boots I slid through the snow without much "hesitation," and Anne fairly flew on the one slick runner of her alpenstock toboggan. Once at the bottom of the long drift we were in the parkland only a short distance above camp. We had come down the entire moraine in one grand slide. We had accomplished in almost no time what would take the Professor some twenty minutes, for we could just see him, high above, picking his way down the series of rock cliffs adjacent to our coasting drift.

When the Professor had finally descended by his arduous rock route our little trio proceeded at once down through the flower-decked parkland, Anne busily collecting botanical specimens, the Professor polishing his spectacles, and I scrawling in my diary some hieroglyphics which to this day I have never completely deciphered. However, I need no notes to recall the wonders of that day. The one word Carbon brings back all —the climb, the glissade, if it indeed merits that name, and the glacier, which, though only the third of Tahoma's glaciers in point of length, differs from all the others in its unique structure and its marvelous history.

Chapter IV

Up the Carbon—Winthrop Cleaver.

Official Climb of the Mazamettes.

In August the Mazama bulletin announced a trip to the Winthrop Glacier. According to announcement the party would start at about nine o'clock in the morning. The territory appealed to the Professor, but not the hour set for starting. With characteristic independence he trudged out of camp on this particular morning at a very few minutes after seven, ostensibly bound for the Winthrop. The rest of us all tagged along —the same crowd that had penetrated to the back neves of the Carbon the day before the "Mazamettes," as we had come to call ourselves.

Once more, as on the previous day, we climbed to the level of the east Moraine of the Carbon; but then, instead of descending the west side, we climbed to the south—east, graduaI]y descending the Winthrop side of the moraine. Where we made good time for there was little real climbing to be done. We merely skirted the Winthrop side of the ridge, keeping at a fairly constant altitude as we crossed alternate stretches of loose, slab shaped rock and cirque like hollows filled with snow.

At about ten o'clock, when the sun had risen high enough to glare down on us with all its intensity from above the Sourdough Range, we reached the ice fields marking the confines of the Winthrop. Here we waited a few minutes to fortify with goggles and grease our eyes and faces against the merciless onslaught of old Sol. Then, looking not unlike a theatrical troupe, we crunched out on the snow—covered surface of the Winthrop. The prospect of St. Elmo's Pass and Steam Boat Prow, and the vast length of the pearly white Winthrop was indeed awe—inspiring. But the truly interesting chasms in the ice appeared to be some distance off; on the other hand, the great snow-banked apex of the Carbon—Winthrop Cleaver seemed to tower almost directly above us on the north—west.

The sight of that enticing pinnacle proved too much for the Professor. Several times I had noticed him pause and gaze with longing eyes toward its summit. At length, with his usual cry of "Water!" he collected the Mazamettes around a well in the ice. At this typical glacier oasis we held formal council regarding our future route. The plea to ascend the Cleaver at length swayed the rest. "Only an hour off" he declared waving his arm dramatically at the sharp rock summit which did look only a short distance above - just beyond the snow bank we were beginning to climb. Once more we slipped hands into our rope nooses and began crunching our "Berg-ab" way over the snow.

The climb up this snow stretch, though fairly steep, was readily negotiable, for the honey—combed structure of the snow furnished us with sound footing. Then, too, we ascended with very little lost motion since the snow had not yet done its work in softening the butter—cups in the snow. Once above the snow field we discovered the "stretch of rock" we had seen below to be a very considerable promontory but not the summit of the Cleaver. What from below had appeared to he a loose shale bed, we now found to be a series of lofty rock cliffs of very interesting structure.

These great cliffs silently tell a marvelous story to the eye that can read the language of the rock. The account of those gigantic cataclysms accompanying the birth of this world—famous volcano are plainly graven here in the geologist's favorite hieroglyphics. At first glance we anticipated little difficulty in scaling the cliffs because of the great size and apparent stability of the boulders composing them. However, a very few moments of climbing showed us a very real danger lurked in these great stones. Every now and then an apparently firm rock of great size would crumble to pieces at a thrust from the alpenstock and rattle down the steep slope in a cloud of dust. On closer examination I found these cliffs to be a veritable agglomeration, part lava and part the rock—like volcanic breccia common to several parts of the Rockies. The presence of lava makes these cliffs extremely treacherous to climb over, because they are so extensively "jointed". In the act of cooling these lava blocks have contracted to such an extent that the cohesion of large boulders has not been sufficient to prevent their breaking up or becoming cracked into the joints mentioned above. Consequently, in climbing over the rotten spine of the Cleaver each Mazamette had to proceed with extreme caution to prevent any rock from falling on the climbers behind. During part of the ascent we climbed, not in line but side by side, thus lessening the danger from falling rock.

After a light lunch at noon we pushed on up the last snow fields to the very buttress of the Cleaver. Over this jagged ridge it was hardly an hours climb to Avalanche Camp, a rotten pinnacle of rock beyond which an impassable gap cuts off the Cleaver from the ridge leading o to the north summit of the mountain, thus rendering farther ascent toward Liberty Cap impossible. The prospect from this crazy rock summit was indeed fearful in its stupendousness. To the south—east there was a sheer drop of many hundred feet to the ice chasms of the Winthrop. On the other side, far below us lay the beautiful Carbon Glacier stretching far to the north toward the cut which it one time carved between the Sluiskin Range and the Mother Mountains. Ahead of us, slightly to the right towered Willis Wall - grim and shaded except for a glorious band of sunlight stretching from Liberty Cap downward some distance on the steep front of the wall.

For some time we stayed at Avalanche Camp, patiently waiting for the sun to release some of the giant drifts which seemed but waiting a little touch to send them thundering from the base of Liberty Cap to the head neves of the Carbon, thousands of feet below. But that little touch was not to be given. Time and again the dull rumble of a rock slide would direct our attention to where clouds of dust were rising, but the hanging snow banks on the summit seemed as stable as granite. At length cameras were folded up and we started the return journey. This proved to be much easier than the ascent, for the rays of the sun had so softened the snow that we were able to descend safely over stretches over which it would have been foolhardy to venture before. Once off the rotten pumice-like lava of the higher cleaver we descended over the snow banks with great rapidity, taking strides that would have made even John Lee's kind of a mountain goat look foolish. Anne even attempted to glissade once or twice, but we passed over no sliding grounds equal to that of the day before.

When we finally tramped into camp we came as confessed outlaws, and as such the Mazamettes were dubbed by our old friend Riley at the camp fire. That night after supper, when all had gathered around the flowing logs (everybody on everybody else s blanket) the Professor arose and duly confessed for himself and his fellow outlaws that the ascent of the Cleaver was made primarily to test the accuracy of' a certain goat story told the night before by John Lee, the veteran goat seer, who can behold that animal where all other eyes see naught. That story was of a certain mother goat and her two kids, -— but that is John Lee's story, not mine.

Chapter V

The Ascent of the Mountain (Rainier)

In making the main climb of the Mountain the Professor and I met with only one real disappointment and that was not of a heart breaking sort. We merely had to part company with the rest of our fellow Mazainettes, for they went ahead with Mr. Gleson while the Professor, at President Prouty's request, staid behind to head a rope line of somewhat less experienced climbers. We did not leave camp till almost ten o' clock, but even then we were far from the last rope line out.

The first stretch of the climb was essentially rock work, for we gradually rounded the great Cleaver of volcanic rock and shale which lifts its giant head Liberty Cap —almost two miles above Moraine Park. The ascent here was necessarily slow, for our way lay over loose rock which can be dislodged very easily to start avalanches of small but very menacing character. After some three hours of this uncertain rock climbing we came suddenly upon a small plateau, green with mountain heather and rendered all the more beautiful by a savage little torrent of glacial water which surged through it. Here we lunched hastily and then pushed on, soon encountering the lower snow neves of the Winthrop, the vast glacier over which our entire climb was to be made.

The Winthrop Glacier is one of the largest and most impressive ice rivers of all the many which Mount Rainier possesses but unfortunately it is seldom seen for it lies out of the beaten path of tourist travel - far to the north - where only the hardy mountaineer dares go alone. The glacier extends from Columbia Crest, the highest summit of the mountain, all the way down to timber line. One might think the ascent of the Mountain by this route would be a matter of little trouble. It is, on the contrary, one of the most difficult ways of conquering the Mountain, for the upper ice fields of the glacier are fearfully precipitous. Besides offering every kind of obstacle in the way of ice climbing - seracs and yawning chasms ,they are honey-combed with hidden crevasses. Most seasons the glacier is not negotiable in its upper reaches but unusually heavy snow last winter made possible our climb, for some of the heretofore impassable crevasses were thus snow-bridged and made fairly safe.

Before starting over the ice fields of the glacier we of course roped up, as did the members of the other groups. When the writer had fastened our group of climbers together so that some six feet of slack rope was left between each, we greased our faces with thick paint and slipped on amber goggles to prevent sun blister and snow blindness. Then Dr. Wynn, the leader of our line gave the word to start. For four hours our course lay over ridge after ridge of crevasses, all sizes, shapes, and depths. Some we avoided by long de tours, some we crossed by means of light wooden ladders, some we jumped, and still others we had to descend, cutting steps down one side and up the other. At twenty minutes after five in the evening we once more encountered rock a comparatively small shale wedge called "Steamboat Prow" - the last rock that our feet would touch before climbing the crater rim at the top of the Mountain.

On the Prow Dr. Wynn and the writer hastily hollowed out with an ice ax a small ledge in the loose rock. After a meager lunch we rolled into our blankets and began what proved to be a night of shivering. About the only thing which made that arctic night watch at all agreeable was the rising of the evening star above the billowy sea of' cloud below us, and it was a "sublime sweet evening star" indeed.

At five o'clock the next morning we shook off the stupor which had been our substitute for sleep. Our breakfast was an abbreviated affair consisting of semi— liquid breakfast food and cocoa. So at very little after five our rope line was once more on its way up the steep ice slopes. Very soon after all the rope lines were well away from Steamboat Prow an incident occurred which demonstrated most graphically of what importance the rope is in glacier climbing. A snow bridge suddenly broke through in the midst of Mr. John Lee's line - the one immediately after ours, Fortunately the crevasse thus opened though six feet wide and some eighty feet deep, was not directly under any member of' the rope line, although eight feet of slack rope between Mr. F. B. Riley and Miss Ethel Freeman passed across the gap. Those in the rope line ahead of Miss Freeman supported her while she leaned back over the crevasse, thus giving Mr. Riley enough slack to loosen the noose about his waste. He then un-roped, crossed the snow bridge at a sounder point, and rejoined his party. If one of the climbers on the rope line had fallen into the opening it would have meant a terrific jerk to him and the other members of his line - but only that however, the same drop would probably have been fatal to a man not supported by the climber's noose.

From steamboat Prow our climb was over gorgeous blue ice walls — some of them seraced in the most fantastic of formations. Again and again we were compelled to make wide de tours to avoid the tell—tale sunken places in the ice which hint of hidden crevasse caverns underneath. Some six hours of constant battling with the crevasse difficulty brought us to an altitude of some fourteen thousand feet. The real Mountain seemed to have saved the worst till the last, with almost human understanding. The last three crevasses we rounded before negotiating the rim of the crater were truly arctic in dimensions. They appeared especially terrible to some of the members of our party who had begun to feel the disconcerting sensations of' mountain sickness.

At the rim of the crater we un-roped and warmed ourselves for a brief moment by the steam vents. The remainder of the climb about four hundred feet - was not very steep and required no rope. Many of us pushed on gradually to the snow mound which marks Columbia Crest, the highest summit of the mountain. But Dr. Wynn was forced to remain at the steam vents for almost an hour with a young man who suffered acutely with mountain sickness. The doctor finally succeeded in getting his patient to the very apex of the Crest, however, and you can well imagine the cheer that greeted his efforts.

Having gazed for a few moments at the summits of Mt. Rood, Mt. Adams, and Mt. St. Helens, just visible above the low-1yng cloud banks which partially obscured the earth, we hastened out of the terrific wind to a point behind the crater rim. There, with Pluto's fires warming us, we ate our lunches and signed the register books.

At one-thirty in the afternoon we began the hazardous glacier descent, having been in the summit since twenty-five minutes of twelve. To the novice at mountaineering the descent always seems to present few difficulties. But the practiced climber will as a rule concede that the most dangerous part of an ice climb is the descent; for this part of the climb is usually made in the afternoon, when climbers are tired and likely to be careless and when the sun has had a chance to do its deadly work on the ice. In descending the vast length of the Winthrop we were startled, and even appalled at times, to note how very materially the condition of the glacier had changed, even since our trip up in the morning. Snow bridges over which we had cut our way safely in the morning were in many instances too rotten to trust, and in other places they had completely disappeared. Consequently our route down was almost entirely new. Time and again we would sink almost to our wastes in loose snow, and one member of our rope line was dismayed to have an alpenstock, which be prized highly, sink completely out of sight at his very feet. A slight investigation showed it to have fallen into a hidden crevasse.

Though descending an ice peak is accompanied by all the dangers of the ascent, it does not tax the climber with short breath. So we were able to travel with quite a bit more alacrity in returning from the summit. We reached Steamboat Prow safely by twenty minutes after five, and from there we proceeded with more confidence over the lower reaches of the glacier. The sun's rays had left this territory and the nightly freezing had already begun. At half past seven we staggered into camp. Tired but exulting over our victory, we collected at the commissary tent. Then the triumphant yell of the "goats" rent the air:

Wah – Who – Wah!

Wah – Who – Wah!

Billy Goat, Nanny Goat,

Ma – Za – Ma

Chapter VI

EXTRA: AUTHENTIC ACCOUNT OF THE WORLD & FAMOUS GLESON EXPEDITION TO GRAND PARK

PRELUDE

History hath shown in the case of many of the world's greatest explorers, man is cruelly skeptical and incredulous in his attitude toward the explorer, who, having penetrated the vast Unknown, lives to tell the tale. Consider the sad case of worthy Dr. Cook. Having hazarded his life he returned from his successful quest of the Pole only to find his countrymen unwilling to believe. Little wonder is it, then, that the famed Rodney Gleson and. his following were laughed to scorn, even by their fellow Mazamas, when they returned from that dark land of mystery -- Grand Park, in the Mt. Rainier National Park Yet, though the present generation looks askance at the startling tale told by the fearless Rodney, Time will show the truth of his assertions. In years to come when the marvels of Grand Park have become common talk and by—words of the street

---then can we imagine the world's great explorers and naturalists convening in solemn conclave to pay tribute to the memory of the immortal Gleson and his band.

So, gentle reader, laugh if you will at this account of the strange prodigies of nature inhabiting Grand Park. In years to come necessity will force you to laugh in a different keys TEMPUS DICET!

FORMAL NARRATIVE

By T. T. Jim, Ph. D., I. W. W., P. Q. D., S. O. S., E. T. C. Ananiasville University

On that memorable morning of August the sun had scarce sent its first glimmer o'er the crest of the Sourdough into Moraine Park when the fearless band of the intrepid Gleson assembled preparatory to making their death-defying dash into Grand Park. All were calm, grim, and determined - all bright of eye save T. T. Jim, who had spent the weary watches of the previous night in what proved to be futile attempts to ease the suffering of fated Lady Robinson.

At five o'clock the explorers silently skirted the north shore of Mystic Lake and then plunged into the forest to the north—east. Knowing not at what moment an earthquake chasm might open to swallow them, or a forest fire blaze forth to scorch them to a crisp, they pushed on, undaunted. Ere long new difficulties presented themselves. The fearless hand found itself obliged to venture out on the unexplored moraines of the lower Winthrop. The terrors of these vast cliffs no tongue can tell. An accurate account would seem but wanton exaggeration; so the writer refrains from attempting a task from which even a literary master might shrink.

Before the morning was old the little band paused to partake of a meagre repast and then dauntlessly resumed the conquest of the unknown. For a time they scaled over jagged rock shelves and crawled 'neath hanging cliffs along the shore of a torrent, the bed of which completely dwarfs the Grand Canyon of the Arizona. Then into a trackless forest they wended their way, clambering 'mid fallen trunks of titanic trees, and avoiding as best they could the poisonous vegetation which flourished in great profusion.

At length, coming once more to the canyon bank, they beheld the first wonder of this journey of wonders, — a giant serpent, a truly terrible monster which lay rhythmically describing figure eights on a ledge of rock. Boa-constrictor—like in size it had an ugly diamond-shaped head, below which the explorers beheld what they thought to be a venom pouch. But this idea was at once discouraged when the reptile spat forth a stream of tobacco juice Yes, mirabile dictu, a tobacco—chewing snake And, what was more, a master chewer; never before had any of the party beheld the weed so skillfully ejected from any mouth except that of the master chewer, old man Longmire himself.

But their exclamations of amazement changed straight way to those of fear when the great reptile suddenly spied and charged them, shooting forth his diamond head with a menacing gesture. Destruction seemed imminent to the helpless band until the resourceful Howard came to the rescue by casting to the irate monster a sack of Bull Durham. With a hiss of delight the snake glided out of sight bearing the sack in its jaws. See footnote.

Footnote: This snake, later captured by Barnes, was exhibited at the Sells-Floto Mazama Circus on Aeroplane Ridge.

Terribly shaken by this near—tragedy the explorers turned their ash—grey faces once more toward the steep, fire-swept bluff, up which lay their way, on top of which lay the strange land of Grand Park with all its untold wonders. Yes, gentle reader, they finally reached that crest but only after climbing some twenty—five thousand feet up cliffs so steep that in places the use of eyebrows was imperative for the explorers to adhere to the treacherous [rock]. When once at the base of the final hillock, only some twenty—five feet below the summit, they beheld a great, bird-like figure palpitating in its death agony on the crest.

Thus they discovered the second marvel of this wild expedition. With their scientific interest at once aroused they proceeded with extreme caution. Though the fowl slightly resembled a grouse at first glance, they found on closer inspection, that it was a griffon of the type long thought to be extinct. It had evidently been pursued by a cougar or wild man, both of which types of animal life are common in Grand Park. See note.

Note: F. A. Cook exhibited both cougar and wild man at the Sells-Floto-Mazama Circus. The wild man displayed was the famed Boscoe.

The convulsion in which the creature was writhing when first sighted by the band proved fatal. The rarity of the atmosphere at that great height made life impossible for the poor griffon. Having prepared a description of this animal monstrosity to send to their esteemed friend, Dr. Cook, President of the Cook Society of Geographical Research and Invention, the explorers proceeded to a point some distance from the front of the crest.

It was here, gentle reader, that fortune favored them with the sight of an animal, which, when captured, proved to be worth the entire Smithsonian Institute. The following narrative of the remarkable is officially approved. Having finished lunch the intrepid climbers were lounging about their fire when one of the party beheld a hard boiled egg move steadily from where it had lain by the fire toward a bush not far off. Doubting his own eyes he shouted to his companions who soon discovered the cause of the startling phenomenon. A huge ant -- as large as a humming bird -- had hold of one end of the egg and was towing the thing away with little difficulty. The astounded climbers gave chase, but to no avail: the prodigious insect succeeded in making off with its forage. Imagine what consternation the discovery of this animal awoke in the explorers! If these were the ants of Grand Park, what in heaven's name might be the flies, gnats, or mosquitoes? Di Immortales! Fancy being attacked by a swarm of robin—sized mosquitoes. The intrepid band hastily broke camp and began to follow the edge of the plateau in an effort to find a point of egress farther down.

Suddenly a cry and a gesture from one of the party directed the attention of the party to another horrible presage, a fair-sized tree — or the remnant of one - which had been gnawed in two by a beaver. But, horror of horrors, the beaver's teeth had done their work at a point on the trunk some twenty-five feet from the ground!

With reckless haste the explorers charged along the plateau rim, at length starting down through almost impassable shrubbery. Down, ever down they scrambled following what in a normal country would pass for deer tracks, but which were doubtless the footprints of a Grand Park squirrel or chipmunk.

After seeming centuries of this blind descent, the explorers stumbled suddenly into a hollow where the roar of falling water deadened all other sound. Glancing up they beheld the now world-famous Lodi Falls. The waters of this colossal cataract fall so many thousand feet that only mist floats down into the gorge below. This, however, rapidly condenses in the shadowed chasms of the canyon. Tumbling seas of water rumble on down to join the main stream in its mad descent from the ice barriers of the Winthrop. Down this tearful gulch the little band wormed its way, now clinging fly-like to shear walls, now perilously shooting the rapids on rotating logs through many stretches even worse than the tamed hell's Half Mile in the Grand Canyon of the Arizona. At length Fate looked with compassion on their tribulations, and guided them to where a chimney-like cut in the rock permitted them to climb out of the canyon and its terrors. Once having gained the mountain side again they plunged down once wore — down with all the recklessness of despair, for the day was well spent and who would relish spending a night where an attack from mosquitoes might prove fatal?

But the explorers were destined to live and publish their epoch—making discoveries to the world. Despite the horrors of the unknown wild they emerged at last on the familiar banks of White River. Thence they trudged hastily over the route they had come, averaging fifteen to twenty miles an hour.

The monotony of this uniform pace began to have a dangerously soporific effect upon Test Tube Jim, whose repose had been none too sound the night before. Yes, only too true, T. T. Jim became too sleepy to be cautious. In a moment of inattention he thrust one foot into a crevice between two rocks. One sharp snap – and his climbing faculties were very seriously impaired. For a while he stumped along, more somnambulist than climber, only to sink at last in a "common-dose" state. Even the most cursory examination of the leg revealed that it was fractured in some twenty-three places. Black as the situation looked for T. T. Jim, Anne, the ever-ready, the infallible guardian angel of the Mazamas came to the rescue. With a few skillful osteopathic maneuvers on the forehead of the fallen warrior she re-summoned fleeting consciousness, and straight-way the bone knitted firmly together in the twenty-three broken parts. Then, for the first time in his life, T. T. realized the truth of those beautiful lines which Walter Scott weaves into his "Marmion" just after that warrior has fallen fatally wounded.

Once on his feet T. T. was himself again and the little band once more hurried on, arriving a very few minutes later at the shore of Mystic Lake, around which a moment's walk brought them into the midst of their comrades. A Te Deum was at once sung in gratitude for the success of the epoch—making feat of exploration, and then a swarm of newspaper men surrounded the little group. After interviewing, a few thousand of these the explorers retired to their tents for a moment's rest in which to prepare descriptions of the animal monstrosities of the trip to send to the Smithsonian Institute and the Cook Society of Geographical Research and Invention.

Thus ended what will doubtless prove to be the greatest feat of exploration of the twentieth century. Of course, if you are a scientist, I have no doubt that the verity of this account will already have become unmistakably obvious to you. However if you are only of the "common herd" to whom these deeds must seem absurd, my one and only word to you is stated in the preface to this article - TEMPUS DICET!!!!

Finis.

www.ingramcontent.com/pod-product-compliance
Ingram Content Group UK Ltd.
Pitfield, Milton Keynes, MK11 3LW, UK
UKHW041929190726
13854UKWH00004B/1530